MySQL
Interview Questions And Answers

X.Y. Wang

Contents

5 Expert 111

Chapter 1

Introduction

As the world becomes increasingly data-driven, the demand for skilled professionals who can manage and manipulate data has grown exponentially. MySQL, one of the most popular open-source relational database management systems, is at the forefront of this data revolution. It is a powerful, reliable, and efficient tool used by organizations of all sizes across various industries to manage and analyze their data. As a result, proficiency in MySQL is a highly sought-after skill among employers, and it can open doors to rewarding and challenging career opportunities.

"MySQL: Interview Questions And Answers" is an expertly crafted book designed to help you prepare for interviews that require knowledge of MySQL. This book serves as both an interview preparation guide and a valuable reference for those looking to advance their careers as database professionals. It provides a comprehensive and organized approach to mastering the key concepts of MySQL, with practical examples and clear explanations that make even the most complex topics accessible.

The book is divided into five progressive sections: Basic, Intermediate, Advanced, Expert, and Guru. Each section builds upon the previous one, ensuring a steady progression of your understanding and mastery of MySQL. The questions in this book span a wide range of topics, from the fundamentals of MySQL and relational database management systems to advanced concepts like query optimization, replication, and performance tuning. By covering such a broad spectrum of topics, this book ensures that you are well-equipped to face any MySQL-related question in an interview setting.

In the Basic section, you will find essential questions about MySQL's main features, data types, keys, and basic SQL statements. This section provides the foundation for understanding MySQL's structure and functionality.

The Intermediate section delves deeper into MySQL's capabilities, with questions on subqueries, storage engines, transactions, constraints, and more. This section will strengthen your understanding of the core concepts while introducing you to some of MySQL's more advanced features.

As you move to the Advanced section, you will encounter questions related to query optimization, partitioning, replication, performance schema, and security. This section prepares you for tackling the more complex and nuanced aspects of MySQL.

In the Expert section, you will find questions on MySQL's performance and scalability, its interaction with other database systems, and advanced techniques for schema design and query optimization. These questions will challenge your understanding of MySQL and help you develop a deeper appreciation for its capabilities.

Finally, the Guru section offers questions on the internals of MySQL, advanced strategies for performance and security, emerging trends in database management, and the role of MySQL in hybrid and multi-cloud environments. This section is designed to test your expertise and help you become a true MySQL guru.

Whether you are a database administrator, developer, or an aspiring database professional, "MySQL: Interview Questions And Answers" will provide you with the knowledge and confidence you need to excel in any MySQL-related interview. This book is your ultimate guide to mastering MySQL and advancing your career in the world of data management. So, let's begin your journey towards becoming a MySQL expert!

Chapter 2

Basic

2.1 What is MySQL, and what are its main features?

MySQL is an open source relational database management system (RDBMS) that is widely used for web applications and for processing data in general.

The main features of MySQL are:

1. Scalability: MySQL can handle large amounts of data efficiently and can be easily scaled to handle even more as needed.

2. Performance: MySQL is designed to be fast, with optimizations for high-speed operations such as data reads and writes.

3. Security: MySQL offers a number of security features to protect data, including encryption, access controls, and auditing.

4. Flexibility: MySQL supports a variety of programming languages, operating systems, and hardware platforms, making it a versatile choice for developers.

5. Replication: MySQL can replicate data across multiple servers for

improved fault tolerance and reliability.

6. Extensibility: MySQL is highly extensible, with a large number of plugins and extensions available, as well as support for custom storage engines and APIs.

7. Community support: MySQL has a large and active community of users, developers, and contributors who continually improve and extend the platform.

8. Cost-effectiveness: MySQL is open source and free to use, making it an affordable choice for small businesses and startups.

Overall, MySQL is a powerful and versatile database system that offers a wide range of features and benefits for developers and businesses alike. Its popularity and widespread adoption make it a safe, reliable, and future-proof choice for storing and managing data.

2.2   What is a relational database management system (RDBMS)?

A relational database management system (RDBMS) is a software system that manages relational databases. In a relational database, data is stored in tables, where each table consists of rows and columns. A row represents a collection of related data, and a column represents a specific attribute or field of the data.

The RDBMS enables users to interact with the database by supporting various operations such as insertion, deletion, and modification of data, as well as running queries that retrieve data from the database. The RDBMS also enforces data integrity and consistency by enforcing constraints and relationships between tables.

Some popular examples of RDBMS include MySQL, Oracle, Microsoft SQL Server, and PostgreSQL. These systems use a common language called Structured Query Language (SQL) to manipulate data in the database.

In summary, an RDBMS is a software system that manages relational databases by supporting various data operations and enforcing data integrity and consistency.

2.3 Can you explain the difference between SQL and MySQL?

SQL (Structured Query Language) is a programming language used to manage and manipulate relational databases. It is a standard language that allows users to create, modify, and query databases. SQL is used in many database management systems (DBMS) such as MySQL, Oracle, Microsoft SQL Server, and PostgreSQL.

MySQL is a popular open-source relational database management system that uses SQL to manage its databases. MySQL was developed by Swedish developers and is now owned by Oracle Corporation. It is used by many websites and applications to store and retrieve data.

Thus, SQL is a language used to manipulate relational databases, while MySQL is a specific relational database management system that uses the SQL language.

Here is an example of SQL code used to create a table in a MySQL database:

```
CREATE TABLE customers (
  id INT PRIMARY KEY,
  name VARCHAR(50),
  email VARCHAR(50)
);
```

This code creates a table named "customers" with three columns: "id", "name", and "email". The "id" column is the primary key column, which means that it will contain a unique identifier for each row in the table. The "name" and "email" columns are VARCHAR columns, which means they can hold up to 50 characters of text.

Overall, SQL is the language used to manage relational databases, and MySQL is one specific DBMS that uses SQL.

2.4   What are the main data types used in MySQL?

In MySQL, there are several data types that can be used to store different types of data. These data types can be classified into the following categories:

1. Numeric data types: These data types are used to store numeric values. Some examples of numeric data types are:

- TINYINT: 1-byte integer, ranged from -128 to 127 or from 0 to 255 (unsigned)

- SMALLINT: 2-byte integer, ranged from -32,768 to 32,767 or from 0 to 65,535 (unsigned)

- MEDIUMINT: 3-byte integer, ranged from -8,388,608 to 8,388,607 or from 0 to 16,777,215 (unsigned)

- INT: 4-byte integer, ranged from -2,147,483,648 to 2,147,483,647 or from 0 to 4,294,967,295 (unsigned)

- BIGINT: 8-byte integer, ranged from -9,223,372,036,854,775,808 to 9,223,372,036,854,775,807 or from 0 to 18,446,744,073,709,551,615 (unsigned)

- DECIMAL: Fixed-point decimal, with configurable precision and scale

2. Date and time data types: These data types are used to store date and time related values. Some examples of date and time data types are:

- DATE: Date value, with format as "YYYY-MM-DD"

- TIME: Time value, with format as "HH:MM:SS"

- DATETIME: Date and time value, with format as "YYYY-MM-DD HH:MM:SS"

- TIMESTAMP: Timestamp value, with format as "YYYY-MM-DD HH:MM:SS"

3. String data types: These data types are used to store string values. Some examples of string data types are:

- CHAR: Fixed-length string, with configurable length

- VARCHAR: Variable-length string, with configurable maximum length

- TEXT: Variable-length string, with maximum length of 65,535 characters

- BLOB: Binary large object, with maximum length of 65,535 bytes

4. Other data types: There are some other data types that can be
used to store specific types of data. Some examples of other data
types are:

```
- ENUM: Enumeration, with a defined set of possible values
- SET: Set of values, each of which can be either present or absent
- BOOLEAN, BOOL: Boolean value, with possible values of TRUE or FALSE
```

Here's an example of how to create a table with different data types:

```
CREATE TABLE my_table (
    id INT NOT NULL AUTO_INCREMENT,
    first_name VARCHAR(50),
    last_name VARCHAR(50),
    age TINYINT UNSIGNED,
    birth_date DATE,
    created_at TIMESTAMP DEFAULT CURRENT_TIMESTAMP,
    is_active BOOLEAN DEFAULT TRUE,
    PRIMARY KEY (id)
);
```

In this example, we have used different data types to define the
columns of the "my_table" table. There is an id column which is
of type INT and has been made as the primary key. The first_name
and last_name columns are of type VARCHAR and can hold string
values of up to 50 characters. The age column is of type TINYINT
UNSIGNED and can hold integer values ranging from 0 to 255. The
birth_date column is of type DATE and can hold date values. The
created_at column is of type TIMESTAMP and has been assigned a
default value of the current timestamp. The is_active column is of
type BOOLEAN and has been assigned a default value of TRUE.

2.5   What is a primary key, and why is it important in a database?

In a relational database, a primary key is a column or set of columns
that uniquely identifies each record in a table. The primary key serves
as a reference point for other tables that need to establish a relationship with the table containing the primary key.

The importance of the primary key lies in its ability to ensure data integrity in the database. By establishing a unique identifier for each record, the primary key helps prevent duplicate or inconsistent data. It also allows for efficient querying and sorting of data in the table.

For example, let's consider a table called "employees" that contains the following columns:

```
| employee_id | first_name | last_name | department_id | hire_date |
|-------------|------------|-----------|---------------|-----------|
| 1           | John       | Smith     | 1             | 2021-01-01 |
| 2           | Jane       | Doe       | 2             | 2021-02-01 |
| 3           | Bob        | Brown     | 1             | 2020-12-01 |
```

In this table, the primary key could be the "employee_id" column, as each employee has a unique identifier. This means that each employee record can be uniquely identified by their "employee_id". If we tried to insert a record with the same "employee_id" as an existing record, we would receive a constraint violation error, since the "employee_id" is the primary key and must be unique.

Overall, the primary key is a crucial component of a well-designed database, as it ensures data accuracy and maintains the integrity of the overall data model.

2.6   What is a foreign key, and how does it help maintain data integrity?

In a relational database such as MySQL, a foreign key is a column or a set of columns in a table that refers to the primary key of another table. It establishes a relationship between two tables, known as the parent (or referenced) table and the child (or referring) table.

For example, suppose we have two tables: Order and Customer. The Order table has a column named CustomerID, which is a foreign key that refers to the primary key column of the Customer table. This means that each order is associated with a single customer, and that customer is identified by their unique CustomerID in the Customer table.

The use of foreign keys helps maintain data integrity by ensuring that only valid data can be inserted into the child table. It does so in two ways:

- First, a foreign key constraint specifies that the value of the foreign key column in the child table must exist in the primary key column of the parent table. In other words, it ensures that a child table cannot reference a nonexistent parent table row. For example, if the Order table's foreign key value references a CustomerID of 12345, then there must be a corresponding row in the Customer table with a CustomerID of 12345. If not, an error will occur when trying to insert or update data in the child table.

- Second, a foreign key constraint can also specify what happens when a row in the parent table is deleted or updated. This is known as the referential action. For example, if the parent row is deleted, the referential action specifies what to do with the associated child rows. MySQL supports several referential actions, such as CASCADE (delete or update the child rows), SET NULL (set the foreign key values in the child rows to NULL), and RESTRICT (prevent the deletion or update of the parent row).

Therefore, by using foreign keys, we can maintain the integrity of the data in the relational database, ensuring that the data is accurate, consistent and in accordance with the rules of the business logic.

2.7　What are the differences between the DELETE, TRUNCATE, and DROP statements in MySQL?

In MySQL, there are three ways to remove data or tables from a database: DELETE, TRUNCATE, and DROP. Although they all have a similar objective, they differ in how they achieve it, and thus the consequences of their usage.

DELETE Statement:

The DELETE statement is used to remove data from a table based on a specific condition or criteria. We can use the WHERE clause with the DELETE statement to specify which rows to delete. Here is an example:

```
DELETE FROM table_name WHERE condition;
```

The DELETE statement removes rows one by one, which means that it is slower than the TRUNCATE statement. However, it has the advantage of allowing us to specify conditions to remove specific rows.

TRUNCATE Statement:

The TRUNCATE statement is used to remove all the rows from a table without logging the individual row deletions. It also resets the auto-increments counter that is used in the primary key fields. Here is an example:

```
TRUNCATE TABLE table_name;
```

TRUNCATE is faster than DELETE because it removes all the rows in one go, which means that we do not have to remove one row at a time. However, its downside is that it removes all the data, and we cannot specify any conditions or criteria to choose which rows to delete.

DROP Statement:

The DROP statement is used to remove a table or a database completely. If we execute the DROP statement against a table, it removes the table structure and its data, and we cannot recover it. If we execute the DROP statement against a database, it removes the whole database, including all the tables contained in it. Here is an example:

```
DROP TABLE table_name;
```

or

```
DROP DATABASE database_name;
```

DROP is the most drastic form of removing data or tables from a database, and we should use it carefully. Once we execute DROP, the data or database is gone forever.

In summary, the DELETE statement is used to remove specific rows, the TRUNCATE statement is used to remove all the rows from a table and reset the auto-increment counter, and the DROP statement is used to remove a table or a database completely. We should use them appropriately based on our use case requirements.

2.8 What is a database schema, and how does it help organize data?

A database schema is a collection of database objects, such as tables, views, indexes, procedures, and functions, that define the structure and organization of a database. It is the blueprint of the database that outlines how the data is organized and how the various components of the database interact with each other.

The schema helps organize data by providing a clear and consistent framework for the database. It defines the structure of each table, including the names of the columns, their data types, and any constraints or relationships between tables. This makes it easier to manage and maintain the data, as well as to query and analyze it.

For example, suppose we have a database to store information about a library's inventory. The database schema would define the tables for books, authors, vendors, and transactions. Each table would have its own columns, such as book title, author name, ISBN number, publishing date, quantity in stock, and price. The schema would also define the relationships between the tables, such as that each book is written by one or more authors, and each transaction involves a specific book and a specific vendor.

By having a well-defined database schema, we can more effectively manage and manipulate the data in the database. We can easily add or modify records, generate reports, and extract the data we need for analysis or other purposes. It also ensures data integrity and consistency across the entire database.

2.9   What is the difference between CHAR and VARCHAR data types in MySQL?

In MySQL, 'CHAR' and 'VARCHAR' are two commonly used data types for storing character string data.

'CHAR' is a fixed-length data type, which means that it always occupies the same amount of storage for every value, regardless of the content. For example, if you define a column as CHAR(10), it will always occupy 10 characters, even if the actual string stored in the column is shorter. If the string is shorter than the defined length, it will be padded with spaces until it reaches the defined length.

'VARCHAR', on the other hand, is a variable-length data type. It means that the storage space for each value depends on the actual length of the string. For example, if you define a column as VARCHAR(10), it will occupy only the needed space plus one byte to store the length of the string. If the string is shorter than the defined length, it will not be padded with spaces.

In general, 'VARCHAR' is more flexible than 'CHAR', as it saves storage space for shorter strings and can accommodate a larger range of string lengths. However, 'CHAR' may perform slightly better for fixed-length strings, as it requires less processing time to find the exact length of each value.

Here is an example to illustrate the difference:

Let's create two tables, 'char_table' and 'varchar_table', with a column defined as 'CHAR(5)' in the first one, and as 'VARCHAR(5)' in the second one.

```
CREATE TABLE char_table (
    id INT PRIMARY KEY,
    name CHAR(5)
);

CREATE TABLE varchar_table (
    id INT PRIMARY KEY,
    name VARCHAR(5)
);
```

Now let's insert some data into both tables:

```
INSERT INTO char_table (id, name) VALUES (1, 'John');
INSERT INTO varchar_table (id, name) VALUES (1, 'John');
```

If we select the data from both tables, we will see that the 'name'
column in 'char_table' is padded with spaces to reach the defined
length:

```
SELECT * FROM char_table;
+----+------+
| id | name |
+----+------+
|  1 | John |
+----+------+
```

While the 'name' column in 'varchar_table' is not padded, but only
occupies the necessary space:

```
SELECT * FROM varchar_table;
+----+------+
| id | name |
+----+------+
|  1 | John |
+----+------+
```

In summary, the choice between 'CHAR' and 'VARCHAR' depends
on the specific needs of your application. If you know that your string
values will always be fixed-length, 'CHAR' may be a better choice in
terms of performance. However, if you need to store strings of varying
lengths, 'VARCHAR' is more appropriate and saves storage space.

2.10   How do you create a database and table in MySQL?

To create a database and table in MySQL, you need to have access to
a MySQL server and be able to log in to that server with appropriate
privileges to create new databases and tables.

First, log in to the MySQL server using the command line client or
a graphical user interface such as MySQL Workbench. Here is an
example of logging in to a MySQL server using the command line:

```
mysql -u username -p
```

Replace 'username' with the username that you use to log in to the
MySQL server. You will be prompted for a password.

Once you are logged in, you can create a database using the 'CREATE

DATABASE' statement. Here is an example of creating a database called 'example_db':

```
CREATE DATABASE example_db;
```

Next, you can create a table within that database using the 'CREATE TABLE' statement. Here is an example of creating a table called 'users' within the 'example_db' database:

```
USE example_db;

CREATE TABLE users (
  id INT AUTO_INCREMENT PRIMARY KEY,
  name VARCHAR(50),
  email VARCHAR(50),
  created_at TIMESTAMP DEFAULT CURRENT_TIMESTAMP
);
```

In this example, the 'users' table has four columns: 'id', 'name', 'email', and 'created_at'. The 'id' column is the primary key of the table and is an auto-incrementing integer. The 'name' and 'email' columns are both of type 'VARCHAR(50)', which can hold up to 50 characters of text. The 'created_at' column is of type 'TIMESTAMP' and includes a default value of the current timestamp.

Once the table is created, you can start inserting data into it using the 'INSERT INTO' statement. Here is an example of inserting a row into the 'users' table:

```
INSERT INTO users (name, email) VALUES ('John Doe', 'johndoe@example.com');
```

This statement inserts a row with a 'name' of "John Doe" and an 'email' of "johndoe@example.com" into the 'users' table.

That's it! You have now created a database and table in MySQL and inserted data into that table.

2.11   What is a JOIN in MySQL, and what are its different types?

In MySQL, JOIN is a SQL command that combines rows from two or more tables based on a related column between them. It allows us to retrieve data from multiple tables in a single query.

There are four types of JOIN in MySQL:

1. INNER JOIN: The INNER JOIN retrieves only the matching rows from both tables based on a specified condition. It only returns rows from the tables where there is a match in both tables according to the specified condition. The syntax of INNER JOIN is as follows:

```
SELECT column1, column2, ...
FROM table1
INNER JOIN table2 ON condition;
```

Example: Suppose we have two tables, Customers and Orders, with the following data:

```
Customers Table:
+----+----------+-----+
| ID | Name     | Age |
+----+----------+-----+
|  1 | John     | 25  |
|  2 | Mary     | 30  |
|  3 | Peter    | 35  |
+----+----------+-----+

Orders Table:
+-----------+------------+-------+
| OrderID   | CustomerID | Total |
+-----------+------------+-------+
| 1         | 2          | 100   |
| 2         | 3          | 200   |
| 3         | 1          | 150   |
+-----------+------------+-------+
```

To retrieve the customer name and order total for each order, we can use the following INNER JOIN query:

```
SELECT Customers.Name, Orders.Total
FROM Customers
INNER JOIN Orders
ON Customers.ID = Orders.CustomerID;
```

This will result in the following output:

```
+-------+-------+
| Name  | Total |
+-------+-------+
| Mary  | 100   |
| Peter | 200   |
| John  | 150   |
+-------+-------+
```

2. LEFT JOIN: The LEFT JOIN retrieves all the rows from the left table and the matching rows from the right table based on a specified condition. If there is no match in the right table, then NULL values are returned. The syntax of LEFT JOIN is as follows:

```
SELECT column1, column2, ...
FROM table1
LEFT JOIN table2 ON condition;
```

Example: To retrieve all the customers even if they have not placed any orders, we can use the following LEFT JOIN query:

```
SELECT Customers.Name, Orders.Total
FROM Customers
LEFT JOIN Orders
ON Customers.ID = Orders.CustomerID;
```

This will result in the following output:

```
+-------+-------+
| Name  | Total |
+-------+-------+
| John  | 150   |
| Mary  | 100   |
| Peter | 200   |
+-------+-------+
| NULL  | NULL  |
+-------+-------+
```

3. RIGHT JOIN: The RIGHT JOIN retrieves all the rows from the right table and the matching rows from the left table based on a specified condition. If there is no match in the left table, then NULL values are returned. The syntax of RIGHT JOIN is as follows:

```
SELECT column1, column2, ...
FROM table1
RIGHT JOIN table2 ON condition;
```

Example: To retrieve all the orders even if they have no customers associated with them, we can use the following RIGHT JOIN query:

```
SELECT Customers.Name, Orders.Total
FROM Customers
RIGHT JOIN Orders
ON Customers.ID = Orders.CustomerID;
```

This will result in the following output:

```
+-------+-------+
| Name  | Total |
+-------+-------+
| Mary  | 100   |
| Peter | 200   |
| John  | 150   |
+-------+-------+
| NULL  | 250   |
+-------+-------+
```

4. FULL JOIN: The FULL JOIN retrieves all the rows from both

tables based on a specified condition. If there is no match in one of the tables, then NULL values are returned for the other table. However, MySQL does not support the FULL JOIN. We can mimic the FULL JOIN by combining the LEFT JOIN and RIGHT JOIN as follows:

```
SELECT column1, column2, ...
FROM table1
LEFT JOIN table2 ON condition
UNION
SELECT column1, column2, ...
FROM table1
RIGHT JOIN table2 ON condition;
```

Example: To retrieve all the customers and all the orders even if they have no matching records, we can use the following FULL JOIN query:

```
SELECT Customers.Name, Orders.Total
FROM Customers
LEFT JOIN Orders
ON Customers.ID = Orders.CustomerID
UNION
SELECT Customers.Name, Orders.Total
FROM Customers
RIGHT JOIN Orders
ON Customers.ID = Orders.CustomerID
WHERE Customers.ID IS NULL;
```

This will result in the following output:

```
+-------+-------+
| Name  | Total |
+-------+-------+
| John  | 150   |
| Mary  | 100   |
| Peter | 200   |
| NULL  | NULL  |
| NULL  | 250   |
+-------+-------+
```

2.12   What is the purpose of the SELECT statement, and what are its main clauses?

The 'SELECT' statement is used to retrieve data from one or more tables in a MySQL database. It is the most commonly used statement in SQL and it allows you to query data based on certain conditions.

The basic syntax of the 'SELECT' statement is as follows:

```
SELECT column1, column2, ...
FROM table_name
WHERE condition;
```

where: - 'column1', 'column2', ... are the columns that you want to retrieve data from. - 'table_name' is the name of the table that you want to retrieve data from. - 'condition' is an optional clause that allows you to filter the data based on certain criteria.

The main clauses of the 'SELECT' statement are:

1. 'SELECT' clause: The 'SELECT' clause specifies the columns that you want to retrieve data from. It can be used to retrieve all columns or specific columns of a table. You can also use expressions, functions or alias names in the 'SELECT' clause.

2. 'FROM' clause: The 'FROM' clause specifies the table or tables that you want to retrieve data from. You can join multiple tables if you want to retrieve data from more than one table.

3. 'WHERE' clause: The 'WHERE' clause is used to filter data based on certain conditions. You can use comparison operators, logical operators, and functions to create complex conditions to filter data.

4. 'GROUP BY' clause: The 'GROUP BY' clause is used to group rows based on one or more columns. You can apply aggregate functions such as 'SUM', 'MAX', 'MIN', 'AVG', and 'COUNT' to calculate summary data based on groups.

5. 'HAVING' clause: The 'HAVING' clause is used to filter data based on the result of an aggregate function. You can use this clause to apply a condition to the output of a 'GROUP BY' clause.

6. 'ORDER BY' clause: The 'ORDER BY' clause is used to sort the result set in ascending or descending order. You can sort data based on one or more columns.

Here is an example of a 'SELECT' statement that retrieves data from a table called 'employees':

```
SELECT first_name, last_name, salary
FROM employees
WHERE department_id = 1
ORDER BY salary DESC;
```

This statement retrieves the first name, last name and salary of all employees who work in the department with an id of 1, and orders the result set by salary in descending order.

2.13   What is the difference between the WHERE and HAVING clauses in a SELECT statement?

In a 'SELECT' statement, the 'WHERE' and 'HAVING' clauses are used to filter the results based on certain conditions.

The 'WHERE' clause is used to filter the rows that are returned in the result set based on a condition that is applied to one or more columns of the table. It is used in conjunction with the 'SELECT', 'UPDATE', and 'DELETE' statements. The condition can consist of a comparison between two values, a range of values, or a set of values. For example, the following query selects all rows from a table named "customers" where the country is "USA":

```
SELECT * FROM customers WHERE country = 'USA';
```

The 'HAVING' clause is used to filter the groups of rows returned in a result set based on a condition that is applied to the group as a whole. The 'HAVING' clause is used together with the 'GROUP BY' clause. It applies a condition to the groups created by the 'GROUP BY' clause, and only returns those groups that satisfy the condition. For example, the following query selects all countries from the "customers" table and the number of customers from each country who have made more than 5 orders:

```
SELECT country, COUNT(*) FROM customers
GROUP BY country HAVING COUNT(*) > 5;
```

In this query, the 'GROUP BY' clause groups the rows by country, and the 'HAVING' clause filters the groups where the number of customers is greater than 5.

In summary, the 'WHERE' clause filters individual rows based on a condition, while the 'HAVING' clause filters groups of rows based on a condition.

2.14 How do you use aggregate functions like COUNT, SUM, AVG, MAX, and MIN in MySQL?

In MySQL, aggregate functions are used to perform calculations on a set of values and return a single value. These functions are commonly used in SQL queries to summarize data and perform statistical calculations on groups of records.

The syntax for using aggregate functions in MySQL is as follows:

```
SELECT aggregate_function(column_name)
FROM table_name
WHERE condition;
```

Here, 'aggregate_function' can be one of the following:

- 'COUNT': Returns the number of rows that matches the condition.

- 'SUM': Returns the sum of the values in the column that matches the condition.

- 'AVG': Returns the average of the values in the column that matches the condition.

- 'MAX': Returns the maximum value in the column that matches the condition.

- 'MIN': Returns the minimum value in the column that matches the condition.

Let's consider an example where we have a table called "orders" with the following columns: "order_id", "customer_id", "order_date", and "amount".

To count the number of orders in the table, we can use the 'COUNT' function as follows:

```
SELECT COUNT(order_id)
FROM orders;
```

This query will return the total number of orders in the "orders" table.

To calculate the average order amount, we can use the 'AVG' function as follows:

```
SELECT AVG(amount)
FROM orders;
```

This query will return the average value of the "amount" column in the "orders" table.

To find the maximum order amount, we can use the 'MAX' function as follows:

```
SELECT MAX(amount)
FROM orders;
```

This query will return the maximum value of the "amount" column in the "orders" table.

Similarly, to find the minimum order amount, we can use the 'MIN' function as follows:

```
SELECT MIN(amount)
FROM orders;
```

This query will return the minimum value of the "amount" column in the "orders" table.

Aggregate functions can also be used with the 'GROUP BY' clause to perform calculations on individual groups of records. For example, to calculate the total amount for each customer, we can use the 'SUM' function with the 'GROUP BY' clause as follows:

```
SELECT customer_id, SUM(amount)
FROM orders
GROUP BY customer_id;
```

This query will return the total sum of order amounts for each customer in the "orders" table.

2.15   What are MySQL indexes, and why are they important for query performance?

In MySQL, an index is a data structure that helps to retrieve data from a database table more efficiently. It is analogous to an index at the back of a book, which allows readers to quickly locate information without scanning the entire book. Like the book index, the database index achieves speed by organizing data based on a specific key.

MySQL indexes are used to speed up the data retrieval process for SELECT, JOIN, and WHERE clauses in SQL queries. By creating an index on one or more columns, MySQL can locate data more quickly, reducing the amount of time necessary to retrieve data from the database. For example, if we have a database of 1,000,000 rows and we want to retrieve all revenue data for the year 2019, if an index has been created on the revenue and date columns, the query will retrieve the data faster than if there was no index on those columns.

Indexes in MySQL can be created using the CREATE INDEX statement. The following example creates an index named 'idx_revenue_date' on the 'revenue' and 'date' columns of a table named 'sales'.

```
CREATE INDEX idx_revenue_date ON sales(revenue, date);
```

There are different types of MySQL indexes, including:

- B-tree index: This is the default index type in MySQL and is suitable for most queries that use the equals (=) operator in the WHERE clause.

- Hash index: This is suitable for queries that use the equals (=) or IN operator in the WHERE clause.

- Full-text index: This is suitable for text search queries that use the MATCH() AGAINST() syntax in the WHERE clause.

MySQL indexes are essential for query performance because without them, the database would have to scan every row sequentially to find the required data, which can be very slow and expensive in terms of resources. Indexes help to reduce the amount of data MySQL needs to scan to find the data required by the query, thereby significantly improving the performance of the query.

However, it's important to note that indexes come with a trade-off. While they can significantly speed up SELECT queries, they can also slow down INSERT, UPDATE, and DELETE queries because the indexes have to be updated every time a change is made to the table. In addition, indexes can take up a significant amount of disk space, which can impact the overall performance of the database. Therefore, it's important to carefully consider which columns to index and when to create indexes based on the types and frequency of queries executed in the system.

2.16 What is normalization, and what are the different normal forms in database design?

Normalization is a process in database design that ensures the efficiency, integrity and scalability of a database schema. It is a set of rules that govern how a database is organized in order to prevent anomalies, redundancy and inconsistencies, which can lead to data loss, errors and inconsistencies. Normalization is typically divided into a series of normal forms, each of which builds upon the previous one, adding additional constraints on the database design.

The main aim of normalization is to minimize data redundancy (information duplication) in tables, avoid update and deletion anomalies, and promote data consistency. Depending on the level of normalization, we can minimize redundancy to such extent that no data is duplicated in the same table or across different tables.

Here are the different normal forms in database design:

1. First normal form (1NF): This is the most basic level of normalization that a table must adhere to. It states that each column in a table must have atomic values, i.e., each field in a table should have only one value. No repeating groups or arrays are allowed, each field should have its own unique value.

For example, a table which stores customer data can have separate columns for customer name, customer id, and address. The customer name column cannot have a comma separated list of names, one per row.

2. Second normal form (2NF): A table is in 2NF if it is already in 1NF and every non-key attribute in the table is fully functionally dependent on the primary key.

A functional dependency is a relationship between two attributes in a table, such that the value of one attribute determines the value of the other. We say that the second attribute is "functionally dependent" on the first attribute. A table that has a composite primary key (a primary key formed using two or more columns) is considered to be in 2NF if each non-key field is dependent on the entire primary key.

For example, a table which stores vendor orders can have a composite primary key, (order_id, item_id) where the order id is the unique identifier and item id identifies the product being ordered. The order date and quantity depend entirely on the (orde_id, item_id) combination and can't appear in any other table.

3. Third normal form (3NF): A table is in 3NF if it is already in 2NF and no non-key attribute in the table is transitively dependent on the primary key.

Transitive dependency is a situation where a field value in a table depends on other fields that are not part of the primary key. For example, consider that a customer order table as described earlier had product unit price stored in each row. Product unit price depends on the product id, but not directly on the order id. This is transitive dependency, and it is resolved by splitting the table into two tables:

   Order table: order_id, customer_id, order_date

   Order details table: order_id, item_id, unit_price, quantity

Here, the unit price is no longer in the same table as order_id, and the Order details table maintains a one-to-many relationship with the order table.

Normalization can go beyond the third normal form, to include the fourth, fifth and even higher normal forms, depending on the complexity of the database. The higher the normal form, the more normalized and the smaller the resultant tables, with reduced duplication of data.

2.17   Can you explain the concept of ACID properties in database transactions?

ACID stands for Atomicity, Consistency, Isolation, and Durability. These properties are the fundamental building blocks of a reliable transaction processing system.

1. Atomicity: An atomic transaction is a single, indivisible unit of work. Either all operations within a transaction must succeed or the transaction must be rolled back to its initial state. Atomicity ensures that the database remains in a consistent state even if a failure occurs during a transaction.

For example, suppose we transfer $100 from Account A to Account B. An atomic transaction for this operation would include deducting $100 from Account A and adding $100 to Account B. If any of these operations fails, the entire transaction is rolled back, and the original account balances are restored.

2. Consistency: The consistency property ensures that a transaction brings the database from one valid state to another. In other words, all integrity constraints defined on the database must be satisfied before and after the transaction.

For example, a database with a constraint that enforces unique email addresses would not allow two users with the same email address to be inserted. If a transaction attempts to insert two users with the same email address, the transaction will fail, and the database remains in its original state.

3. Isolation: Isolation ensures that concurrent transactions do not conflict with each other. Each transaction should appear to be executing in isolation, independent of other transactions. This property prevents a transaction from seeing the intermediate states of other concurrent transactions, as well as prevents the intermediate states of a transaction from being visible to other transactions.

For example, if two users try to withdraw money from the same account at the same time, isolation ensures that both transactions cannot occur simultaneously. One transaction must complete before the other can start, ensuring that each transaction completes successfully.

4. Durability: Durability ensures that once a transaction is committed, it will remain committed in the face of subsequent failures, including power loss, crashes, or disk failures. The changes made by committed transactions must persist, even if the system fails immediately after the transaction is completed.

For example, if a transaction is committed that transfers funds between accounts, then the result of that transaction must be preserved even if the system crashes before the changes are written to disk. This can be achieved through the use of a transaction log, which records all changes made by transactions and can be used to recover from failures.

To summarize, the ACID properties ensure that database transactions are reliable and consistent, even in the face of failures and concurrent access. They are critical to the integrity of any data-intensive system.

2.18   What is a stored procedure, and what are its advantages?

A stored procedure is a prepared and precompiled block of code that resides in the database and can be executed by invoking a simple call to its name. It is a set of SQL statements that can be stored in a database an executed when needed by applications' calls. Stored procedures are commonly used in database systems such as MySQL.

The advantages of using stored procedures include:

1. Performance improvement: Stored procedures can be precompiled and optimized by the database system, which can significantly improve the performance of the database. Because stored procedures are executed in the database, they can greatly reduce the amount of data that needs to be sent between the application and the database, resulting in faster response times.

2. Security: Stored procedures can be used to restrict access to specific data or functionality within a database. Because users of the database must call the stored procedure rather than accessing the underlying tables directly, it is easier to control access to sensitive information and prevent unauthorized modifications.

3. Reusability: Stored procedures can be reused across multiple applications and databases, which can save time and effort in development.

4. Maintainability: Since stored procedures are centralized and defined within the database, they are easier to maintain and update than code that is scattered across different applications.

5. Transaction control: Stored procedures can be used to ensure that a series of database operations are completed as a single logical transaction. This can help ensure data integrity and consistency.

For example, consider the following simple stored procedure that selects all the customers from a table based on a given country:

```
CREATE PROCEDURE selectCustomersByCountry (IN country varchar(255))
BEGIN
  SELECT * FROM customers WHERE customers.country = country;
END
```

This stored procedure can be called by an application with a simple command like 'CALL selectCustomersByCountry('USA')', which will return all the customers from the USA. The stored procedure can be reused by other applications as well, improving maintainability and reducing development time. Additionally, since the SQL statement in the stored procedure has been precompiled and optimized, this stored procedure may execute faster than the equivalent SQL statement executed directly from an application.

2.19 What is the difference between INNER JOIN and OUTER JOIN in MySQL?

In MySQL, JOIN is used to combine rows from two or more tables based on a related column between them. INNER JOIN and OUTER

JOIN are two types of JOIN used in MySQL.

* INNER JOIN: It returns only those rows for which the join condition is true. In other words, it returns the intersection between the two tables.

The syntax for INNER JOIN is as follows:

```
SELECT *
FROM table1
INNER JOIN table2
ON table1.column = table2.column;
```

Here, table1 and table2 are the names of the tables being joined, and column is the name of the column on which the tables are being joined.

For example, consider two tables 'employees' and 'departments' with the following data:

```
employees table:

id | name | department_id
---|--------|--------------
1  | Alice  | 1
2  | Bob    | 2
3  | Charlie| 1
4  | David  | 3

departments table:

id | name
---|--------
1  | Sales
2  | Marketing
```

To join these two tables with INNER JOIN based on the 'department_id' column, the query would be:

```
SELECT employees.name, departments.name
FROM employees
INNER JOIN departments
ON employees.department_id = departments.id;
```

This would return the following result:

```
name    | name
--------|---------
Alice   | Sales
Charlie | Sales
Bob     | Marketing
```

* OUTER JOIN: It returns all the rows from at least one table, and

the matching rows from the other table. In other words, it returns
the union of the two tables. There are three types of OUTER JOIN:
LEFT OUTER JOIN (or LEFT JOIN), RIGHT OUTER JOIN (or
RIGHT JOIN), and FULL OUTER JOIN (or FULL JOIN).

The syntax for LEFT OUTER JOIN is as follows:

```
SELECT *
FROM table1
LEFT OUTER JOIN table2
ON table1.column = table2.column;
```

Here, table1 and table2 are the names of the tables being joined,
and column is the name of the column on which the tables are being
joined.

For example, to perform a LEFT OUTER JOIN between 'employees'
and 'departments' tables based on the 'department_id' column, the
query would be:

```
SELECT employees.name, departments.name
FROM employees
LEFT JOIN departments
ON employees.department_id = departments.id;
```

This would return the following result:

```
name    | name
--------|---------
Alice   | Sales
Bob     | Marketing
Charlie | Sales
David   | NULL
```

In the result, the rows with NULL value in the 'name' column are the
rows from the 'employees' table that did not match any row in the
'departments' table based on the join condition.

Similar to LEFT OUTER JOIN, we can use RIGHT OUTER JOIN
to return all the rows from the right table, and the matching rows
from the left table. And, we can use FULL OUTER JOIN to return
all the rows from both tables, and the matching rows based on the
join condition.

In summary, INNER JOIN returns only the matching rows between
two tables, while OUTER JOIN returns all the rows from at least one
table, and the matching rows from the other table.

2.20   What is a view in MySQL, and what are its main use cases?

In MySQL, a view is a virtual table that is created based on the result of a SELECT statement, and it does not store any data itself. The query used to create the view is saved as an object in the database and can be used interchangeably with a physical table. The view can be used as if it were a regular table, but it can also be used to abstract or simplify more complex queries.

A view can have columns, just like a regular table, and it can also calculate values based on existing tables or views. Views can be used to restrict access to data for certain users by exposing only relevant data to them. They can also be used to provide an easy-to-use interface for a complex query, making it simple to use the same query repeatedly without having to rewrite it each time.

There are several common use cases for views in MySQL:

1. Data Restriction: Views can be used to restrict access to certain data for different users, allowing them to only see the data that is relevant to their needs.

For example, suppose we have a table named 'employees' that contains information about all employees, including sensitive information like social security numbers. We can create a view that only shows the employee name and hire date to non-admin users, while the admin user could see all the data.

```
CREATE VIEW non_admin_employees AS
SELECT name, hire_date
FROM employees;
```

2. Query Abstraction: Views can be used to simplify complex queries by breaking them down into smaller, more manageable parts. This can make it easier to work with larger datasets.

Suppose we have a database that contains several tables with different types of data. We can create a view that combines the data from these tables into a single, easy-to-use view.

```
CREATE VIEW product_info AS
SELECT products.product_name, suppliers.supplier_name, categories.
    category_name
```

```
FROM products
INNER JOIN suppliers ON products.supplier_id = suppliers.supplier_id
INNER JOIN categories ON products.category_id = categories.category_id;
```

3. Report Generation: Views can be used to generate reports that contain data from one or multiple tables. This can be useful to provide insights into data stored across multiple tables.

For example, suppose that we have three tables 'employees', 'departments', and 'salaries'. We can create a view that displays the total salary for each department, making it easier to generate reports on salary expenses.

```
CREATE VIEW salary_by_dept AS
SELECT departments.department_name, SUM(salaries.salary) as total_salary
FROM employees, departments, salaries
WHERE employees.department_id = departments.department_id AND
employees.employee_id = salaries.employee_id
GROUP BY departments.department_name;
```

In conclusion, views in MySQL can be used to simplify queries, restrict access to sensitive data, and generate reports. They are a useful tool for any database administrator to have in their toolbox.

Chapter 3

Intermediate

3.1 What is a subquery, and how is it used in MySQL?

In MySQL, a subquery is a query that is nested inside another query, and it is used to obtain intermediate results that can be used as an input in the outer query. Essentially, a subquery is a way to combine multiple queries into a single query by using the results of one query as a condition in another query.

The basic syntax of a subquery in MySQL is as follows:

```
SELECT column_name(s)
FROM table_name
WHERE column_name operator (SELECT column_name FROM table_name WHERE
    condition);
```

In this syntax, the subquery ("SELECT column_name FROM table_name WHERE condition") is enclosed in parentheses and used as a condition in the WHERE clause of the outer query.

There are two types of subqueries in MySQL: the single-row subquery and the multiple-row subquery.

A single-row subquery is a subquery that returns only one row of

45

results, and it is typically used as a condition in the WHERE clause
of the outer query. For example, the following query uses a single-row
subquery to retrieve the name of the player with the highest score:

```
SELECT name
FROM players
WHERE score = (SELECT MAX(score) FROM players);
```

A multiple-row subquery, on the other hand, is a subquery that returns multiple rows of results, and it is typically used as a condition in
the WHERE or HAVING clause of the outer query. For example, the
following query uses a multiple-row subquery to retrieve the names
of all players who have a higher score than the average score:

```
SELECT name
FROM players
WHERE score > (SELECT AVG(score) FROM players);
```

In summary, a subquery is a powerful feature of MySQL that allows
you to combine multiple queries into a single query by using the results
of one query as a condition in another query. By using subqueries,
you can write more efficient and compact queries that retrieve exactly
the data you need.

3.2   Can you explain the differences be-
tween MyISAM and InnoDB storage
engines in MySQL?

MySQL supports multiple storage engines, each with its own advantages and disadvantages, and two of the most commonly used ones
are MyISAM and InnoDB.

MyISAM is the default storage engine in MySQL versions prior to
5.5. It's a very simple and efficient storage engine that's ideal for
read-heavy applications.

InnoDB, on the other hand, is a more complex storage engine that's
designed to offer transactional capabilities and better performance for
write-heavy workloads.

Here are some key differences between MyISAM and InnoDB:

1. **ACID compliance**. InnoDB is ACID-compliant, which means that it supports transactions and ensures consistency even in the face of system failures. MyISAM, on the other hand, does not support transactions, so it's not suitable for applications that require this feature.

2. **Locking mechanism**. MyISAM uses table-level locking, which means that only one user can write to a table at a time. InnoDB, on the other hand, uses row-level locking, which allows multiple users to write to the same table simultaneously without interfering with each other. This makes InnoDB a better choice for write-heavy workloads where performance is critical.

3. **Foreign key constraints**. InnoDB supports foreign key constraints, which ensure referential integrity between tables. MyISAM, on the other hand, does not support foreign key constraints, so applications that rely on them must use InnoDB or another storage engine that supports them.

4. **Full-text search**. MyISAM supports full-text search, which allows users to search for text within fields. InnoDB, on the other hand, does not support full-text search natively, although it can be added using external plugins.

5. **Indexing**. MyISAM indexes are stored separately from the data, which can improve performance in read-heavy workloads. InnoDB indexes are stored alongside the data, which can reduce disk I/O and improve performance in write-heavy workloads.

In conclusion, both MyISAM and InnoDB have their own advantages and disadvantages, so the choice of which storage engine to use depends on the specific requirements of the application. If the application requires transactions, foreign key constraints, or concurrent writes to the same table, then InnoDB is a better choice. If the application is read-heavy and requires full-text search, then MyISAM may be a better option.

3.3   What is a transaction, and how do you implement transactions in MySQL using COMMIT and ROLLBACK?

In database systems, a transaction is a sequence of one or more SQL operations that are treated as a single logical unit of work. These operations can include selecting, updating, deleting, or inserting data into a table. Transactions allow these operations to be treated as a single cohesive operation that must either be completed in its entirety or not at all.

In MySQL, transactions can be implemented using the 'COMMIT' and 'ROLLBACK' commands.

When a transaction is started in MySQL, all subsequent SQL statements are treated as part of that transaction until the transaction is either committed or rolled back. Any changes made during the transaction are not immediately made permanent in the database, but are rather held in a temporary state until the transaction is committed. If the transaction is rolled back, any changes made during the transaction are discarded and the database state is returned to what it was before the transaction started.

The basic syntax for implementing a transaction in MySQL is as follows:

```
START TRANSACTION;
-- SQL statements here
COMMIT;
-- or
ROLLBACK;
```

The 'START TRANSACTION' statement begins the transaction, and all subsequent SQL statements are treated as part of the transaction. Once the SQL statements have been executed, the 'COMMIT' statement is used to commit the changes made during the transaction to the database. Alternatively, the 'ROLLBACK' statement can be used to discard the changes and revert the database to its state before the transaction began.

For example, consider the following scenario:

Suppose we have a table 'employees' with columns 'id' and 'salary', and we want to give a bonus to all employees whose salary is above a certain threshold. We can implement this using a transaction as follows:

```
START TRANSACTION;
UPDATE employees SET salary = salary * 1.1 WHERE salary > 50000;
COMMIT;
```

In this example, the 'UPDATE' statement is the SQL operation we want to perform as part of the transaction. The 'START TRANSACTION' statement begins the transaction, and the 'COMMIT' statement at the end of the example commits the changes made by the 'UPDATE' statement to the database.

If, for some reason, we want to roll back the transaction, we can use the following code:

```
START TRANSACTION;
UPDATE employees SET salary = salary * 1.1 WHERE salary > 50000;
ROLLBACK;
```

In this example, the 'ROLLBACK' statement is used to discard any changes made by the 'UPDATE' statement and return the database to its state prior to the 'START TRANSACTION' statement.

In summary, transactions in MySQL are used to ensure that a sequence of SQL statements are treated as a single logical unit of work. This can be accomplished using the 'START TRANSACTION', 'COMMIT', and 'ROLLBACK' statements. The 'COMMIT' statement is used to save any changes made during the transaction to the database, while the 'ROLLBACK' statement is used to discard any changes made during the transaction and return the database to its state before the transaction began.

3.4   What are the different types of MySQL constraints, and how do they help maintain data integrity?

In MySQL, constraints are used to define and enforce rules for the data that is stored in tables. Constraints help ensure data integrity by preventing invalid or inappropriate data from being stored in the table. There are several types of constraints in MySQL, including:

1. NOT NULL Constraint: The NOT NULL constraint ensures that a column cannot have a NULL value. If a user tries to insert or update a row with a NULL value, an error will be thrown.

Example:

```
CREATE TABLE customers (
  customer_id INT NOT NULL,
  name VARCHAR(50) NOT NULL,
  address VARCHAR(100),
  PRIMARY KEY (customer_id)
);
```

2. UNIQUE Constraint: The UNIQUE constraint ensures that a column or combination of columns have unique values. This means that no two rows in the table can have the same value in the specified column(s).

Example:

```
CREATE TABLE employees (
  employee_id INT PRIMARY KEY,
  email VARCHAR(50) UNIQUE,
  phone VARCHAR(20) UNIQUE
);
```

3. PRIMARY KEY Constraint: The PRIMARY KEY constraint ensures that each row in a table is uniquely identified by a specific column or combination of columns. This constraint is used to identify the primary key of a table.

Example:

```
CREATE TABLE orders (
  order_id INT PRIMARY KEY,
  customer_id INT,
  order_date DATE,
  FOREIGN KEY (customer_id) REFERENCES customers(customer_id)
);
```

4. FOREIGN KEY Constraint: The FOREIGN KEY constraint ensures that data in a column matches the values of data in another table's column. It establishes a relationship between two tables.

Example:

```
CREATE TABLE orders (
```

```
order_id INT PRIMARY KEY,
customer_id INT,
order_date DATE,
FOREIGN KEY (customer_id) REFERENCES customers(customer_id)
);
```

5. CHECK Constraint: The CHECK constraint is used to ensure that data in a column meets a specific condition or set of conditions.

Example:

```
CREATE TABLE payments (
  payment_id INT PRIMARY KEY,
  customer_id INT,
  payment_date DATE,
  amount DECIMAL(10, 2),
  CHECK (amount >= 0 AND amount <= 10000),
  FOREIGN KEY (customer_id) REFERENCES customers(customer_id)
);
```

All of these constraints help ensure that data integrity is maintained in a MySQL database. By enforcing rules for the data in table columns, constraints prevent invalid or inappropriate data from being stored in the table.

3.5 How do you perform pagination using the LIMIT and OFFSET clauses in MySQL?

Pagination is a technique of dividing large amounts of data into smaller, more manageable chunks (or pages) to improve the performance of database queries. In MySQL, pagination can be performed using the 'LIMIT' and 'OFFSET' clauses.

The 'LIMIT' clause restricts the number of rows returned by a query, while the 'OFFSET' clause skips a specified number of rows before starting to return records. Together, these two clauses can be used to implement pagination.

Suppose we have a table called 'users' which contains a large number of records that we want to paginate. To limit the number of records returned to 10, and skip the first 20 records, we can use the following query:

```
SELECT * FROM users LIMIT 10 OFFSET 20;
```

In this example, the 'LIMIT' clause restricts the number of records returned to 10, while the 'OFFSET' clause skips the first 20 records. The query will return the 21st to the 30th records from the 'users' table.

A common use case for pagination is to display records on a web page. In this case, we typically need to know the total number of records in the table so that we can calculate the number of pages needed to display all the records.

Suppose we want to display 10 records per page, starting from the first page. We can use the following query to retrieve the first 10 records:

```
SELECT * FROM users LIMIT 10 OFFSET 0;
```

To retrieve the second page of records, we can use the following query:

```
SELECT * FROM users LIMIT 10 OFFSET 10;
```

And so on, until we have retrieved all the records.

To determine the total number of records in the table, we can use the 'COUNT()' function, like this:

```
SELECT COUNT(*) FROM users;
```

This query will return the total number of records in the 'users' table. We can then divide this number by the number of records we want to display per page to determine the total number of pages.

For example, if the 'COUNT()' query returns a value of 100 and we want to display 10 records per page, we need 10 pages to display all the records.

Pagination using the 'LIMIT' and 'OFFSET' clauses is a simple and effective way to improve the performance of database queries when dealing with large amounts of data.

3.6 What is the difference between UNION and UNION ALL in MySQL?

In MySQL, both UNION and UNION ALL are used to combine the result sets of two or more SELECT statements. However, there is a significant difference between these two operators, which is explained below:

1. UNION

UNION is used to combine the result set of two or more SELECT statements, and it only returns unique rows from the final result set. It excludes duplicate rows from the result set by comparing each row in the result set. To use UNION operator, the following conditions must be satisfied:

```
- The number of columns in all SELECT statements must be the same.
- The data types of the corresponding columns in all SELECT statements must
    be compatible.
```

The syntax for using UNION operator is as follows:

```
SELECT column1, column2, column3, ... FROM table1 WHERE condition1
UNION
SELECT column1, column2, column3, ... FROM table2 WHERE condition2;
```

For example, if we have two tables "employees" and "customers", and we want to combine the first name and last name of all employees and customers and return the unique results, we can use the following query:

```
SELECT first_name, last_name FROM employees
UNION
SELECT first_name, last_name FROM customers;
```

2. UNION ALL

UNION ALL also combines the result set of two or more SELECT statements, but it returns all rows from the final result set, including duplicates. It does not remove duplicate rows from the result set. To use UNION ALL operator, the same conditions as for UNION operator needs to be satisfied.

The syntax for using UNION ALL operator is as follows:

```
SELECT column1, column2, column3, ... FROM table1 WHERE condition1
UNION ALL
SELECT column1, column2, column3, ... FROM table2 WHERE condition2;
```

For example, if we want to combine the first name and last name of employees and customers and return all results (including duplicates), we can use the following query:

```
SELECT first_name, last_name FROM employees
UNION ALL
SELECT first_name, last_name FROM customers;
```

In summary, UNION and UNION ALL are used to combine result sets of two or more SELECT statements, but the former returns unique rows while the latter returns all rows (including duplicates).

3.7 How do you use the GROUP_CON-CAT function in MySQL, and what is its purpose?

The 'GROUP_CONCAT' function in MySQL is used to concatenate the values of a column from multiple rows into a single string. The concatenated string is returned as the output of the function.

The general syntax of the 'GROUP_CONCAT' function is as follows:

```
SELECT GROUP_CONCAT(column_name SEPARATOR ',') FROM table_name GROUP BY
    group_column;
```

where 'column_name' is the name of the column whose values need to be concatenated, 'table_name' is the name of the table from which the data is being retrieved, 'group_column' is the name of the column by which the data is being grouped, and 'SEPARATOR' is an optional parameter that specifies the string to be used as a separator between the concatenated values. If the 'SEPARATOR' parameter is not specified, a comma is used as the default separator.

Here is an example of how to use the 'GROUP_CONCAT' function in MySQL. Suppose we have a table named 'employees' with the following data:

```
| id | name  | department |
|----|-------|------------|
| 1  | John  | Sales      |
| 2  | Jane  | HR         |
| 3  | Sarah | Sales      |
| 4  | Mike  | Marketing  |
| 5  | Alex  | Marketing  |
```

If we want to concatenate the names of all employees in each department, we can use the following SQL statement:

```sql
SELECT department, GROUP_CONCAT(name SEPARATOR ',␣') AS employees
FROM employees
GROUP BY department;
```

This will produce the following output:

```
| department | employees     |
|------------|---------------------|
| Sales      | John, Sarah   |
| HR         | Jane          |
| Marketing  | Mike, Alex    |
```

As we can see, the 'GROUP_CONCAT' function has concatenated the names of all employees in each department into a single string, separated by a comma.

The 'GROUP_CONCAT' function can also be used to concatenate values from multiple columns. For example, suppose we have a table named 'orders' with the following data:

```
| id | customer | product | quantity |
|----|----------|---------|----------|
| 1  | John     | iPhone  | 2        |
| 2  | Sarah    | iPad    | 1        |
| 3  | John     | MacBook | 3        |
| 4  | Mike     | iMac    | 2        |
| 5  | Alex     | iPhone  | 1        |
```

If we want to concatenate the 'product' and 'quantity' values for each customer, we can use the following SQL statement:

```sql
SELECT customer, GROUP_CONCAT(product, '␣(', quantity, ')␣' SEPARATOR ',␣')
    AS orders
FROM orders
GROUP BY customer;
```

This will produce the following output:

```
| customer | orders                                 |
|----------|----------------------------------------|
```

```
| John   | iPhone (2), MacBook (3) |
| Sarah  | iPad (1)                |          |
| Mike   | iMac (2)                |          |
| Alex   | iPhone (1)              |          |
```

As we can see, the 'GROUP_CONCAT' function has concatenated the 'product' and 'quantity' values for each customer into a single string, separated by a comma and enclosed in parenthesis.

In conclusion, the 'GROUP_CONCAT' function in MySQL is a powerful tool for concatenating the values of a column from multiple rows into a single string. It is useful for generating summary reports and for simplifying the output of complex queries.

3.8   What are the different types of date and time functions in MySQL?

MySQL provides various date and time functions to manipulate and format date and time values. These functions can be used to perform various computations on date and time values, such as formatting date and time strings, extracting parts of date and time values, performing date and time arithmetic, and converting date and time values between different formats.

Some of the commonly used date and time functions are:

1. 'NOW()': This function returns the current date and time in the format 'YYYY-MM-DD HH:MM:SS'.

Example:

```
SELECT NOW();

Output:
2021-11-30 10:15:30
```

2. 'DATE()': This function extracts the date part from a date or datetime value.

Example:

```
SELECT DATE('2021-11-30 10:15:30');
```

```
Output:
2021-11-30
```

3. 'TIME()': This function extracts the time part from a date or datetime value.

Example:

```
SELECT TIME('2021-11-30␣10:15:30');
```

```
Output:
10:15:30
```

4. 'YEAR()': This function extracts the year part from a date or datetime value.

Example:

```
SELECT YEAR('2021-11-30');
```

```
Output:
2021
```

5. 'MONTH()': This function extracts the month part from a date or datetime value.

Example:

```
SELECT MONTH('2021-11-30');
```

```
Output:
11
```

6. 'DAY()': This function extracts the day part from a date or datetime value.

Example:

```
SELECT DAY('2021-11-30');
```

```
Output:
30
```

7. 'HOUR()': This function extracts the hour part from a time or datetime value.

Example:

```
SELECT HOUR('10:15:30');

Output:
10
```

8. 'MINUTE()': This function extracts the minute part from a time or datetime value.

Example:

```
SELECT MINUTE('10:15:30');

Output:
15
```

9. 'SECOND()': This function extracts the second part from a time or datetime value.

Example:

```
SELECT SECOND('10:15:30');

Output:
30
```

10. 'DATEDIFF()': This function calculates the difference between two dates in days.

Example:

```
SELECT DATEDIFF('2021-11-30', '2021-11-25');

Output:
5
```

11. 'DATE_ADD()': This function adds a specified interval to a date or datetime value.

Example:

```
SELECT DATE_ADD('2021-11-30', INTERVAL 1 MONTH);

Output:
2021-12-30
```

12. 'DATE_SUB()': This function subtracts a specified interval from a date or datetime value.

Example:

```
SELECT DATE_SUB('2021-11-30', INTERVAL 1 MONTH);


Output:
2021-10-30
```

13. 'STR_TO_DATE()': This function converts a string to a date-time value based on a specified format.

Example:

```
SELECT STR_TO_DATE('30/11/2021', '%d/%m/%Y');


Output:
2021-11-30
```

These are some of the commonly used date and time functions in MySQL. There are many more functions available for performing various date and time operations in MySQL.

3.9   How do you use the CASE statement in MySQL, and what are its use cases?

The 'CASE' statement in MySQL is a conditional expression that allows you to perform different actions based on different conditions. It is often used as a replacement for the 'IF' statement when more than two conditions are involved. The syntax for the 'CASE' statement is as follows:

```
CASE case_value
    WHEN when_value THEN result
    [WHEN when_value THEN result ...]
    [ELSE else_result]
END;
```

Here, 'case_value' is the value being evaluated, 'when_value' is the value being tested against, 'result' is the value returned if the condition is true, and 'else_result' is the value returned if none of the conditions are true. The 'CASE' statement can evaluate multiple conditions by using multiple 'WHEN' clauses.

Let's take a look at an example of how to use the 'CASE' statement in MySQL. Suppose we have a table named 'employees' with the following columns: 'id', 'name', 'salary', and 'department'.

```
SELECT name, salary,
  CASE
    WHEN salary >= 5000 THEN 'High'
    WHEN salary >= 3000 THEN 'Medium'
    ELSE 'Low'
  END AS 'Salary Band'
FROM employees;
```

In this query, we are selecting the 'name', 'salary', and a 'Salary Band' that will be calculated using the 'CASE' statement. If an employee's salary is greater than or equal to 5000, the 'Salary Band' will be 'High'. If it is between 3000 and 4999, it will be 'Medium'. Otherwise, it will be 'Low'.

Another use case for the 'CASE' statement is to update a column in a table based on certain conditions. For example, let's say we want to update the 'department' column of the 'employees' table based on their salary. Employees with a salary greater than or equal to 5000 will be assigned to the 'Management' department, while employees with a salary between 3000 and 4999 will be assigned to the 'Staff' department. Employees with a salary less than 3000 will be assigned to the 'Entry Level' department.

```
UPDATE employees
SET department = CASE
    WHEN salary >= 5000 THEN 'Management'
    WHEN salary >= 3000 THEN 'Staff'
    ELSE 'Entry Level'
  END;
```

In this query, we are updating the 'department' column of the 'employees' table using the 'CASE' statement. If an employee's salary is greater than or equal to 5000, they will be assigned to the 'Management' department. If it is between 3000 and 4999, they will be assigned to the 'Staff' department. Otherwise, they will be assigned to the 'Entry Level' department.

In conclusion, the 'CASE' statement in MySQL is a powerful tool that can be used to perform different actions based on different conditions. Its use cases include selecting calculated values in a query and updating columns in a table based on certain conditions.

3.10 What is a prepared statement in MySQL, and why is it important for security?

A prepared statement in MySQL is a feature that allows for the creation of a template SQL statement with placeholders for parameters, which can then be reused multiple times with different input values. The statement is first prepared by the database, and then executed by sending only the input values to the database engine, rather than the entire SQL statement each time.

The benefits of using prepared statements include:

1. Performance Optimization: Prepared statements are compiled and optimized by the database engine only once for every template, which means that it saves time during execution.

2. Prevention against SQL injection: SQL Injection is a common attack that can be used by attackers to steal or modify data from a database. By using prepared statements, we can separate SQL queries from data. Prepared statements automatically take care of data escaping and prevents SQL injection even if input variables contain SQL code.

3. Help in avoiding recompilation: If a database has to handle frequent queries with varying user data, then the prepared statements can be of great help to increase performance because the database does not have to recompile the same SQL code each time.

Here is an example of how to use prepared statements in MySQL using PHP:

Suppose we have a table named "users", and we want to check if a user with a given username and password exists in the database using a prepared statement. The PHP code for this could be written as follows:

```
// 1. Prepare the statement
```

```
$stmt = $conn->prepare("SELECT␣*␣FROM␣users␣WHERE␣username␣=␣?␣AND␣password␣=
    ␣?");

// 2. Bind the parameters
$stmt->bind_param("ss", $username, $password);

// 3. Set the parameters
$username = "johndoe";
$password = "mypassword";

// 4. Execute the statement
$stmt->execute();

// 5. Get the result
$result = $stmt->get_result();

// 6. Process the result
if($result->num_rows === 1) {
    // user exists
} else {
    // user does not exist
}

// 7. Close the statement
$stmt->close();
```

In the above example, we first prepare the SQL statement with place-holders for the parameters we want to bind to the statement. We then bind the parameters to the statement using the 'bind_param()' function, which takes types and values of the parameters. Finally, we execute the statement and retrieve the result using the 'get_result()' function. After processing the result, we close the statement. This example demonstrates the use of prepared statements for preventing SQL injection, as user-supplied data is separated from the SQL code.

3.11   How do you perform backup and restoration of MySQL databases?

Backup and restoration are critical activities for any database system. This ensures the safety of the data and the availability of a copy of the data in case of disasters, hardware failures, or other unforeseen circumstances.

MySQL provides several options for backing up and restoring databases, including the use of mysqldump, the MySQL Enterprise Backup tool, and replication.

Backup with mysqldump:

One commonly used tool for creating backups of MySQL databases is mysqldump. This tool is a command-line program that can be used to dump a database or a set of databases to a file. The dump file contains SQL statements that can be used to recreate the database schema and data.

Here is an example of how to create a backup of a single database using mysqldump:

```
$ mysqldump -u username -p dbname > dbname_backup.sql
```

In this command, username is the username of the MySQL account with privileges on the database, dbname is the name of the database to be backed up, and dbname_backup.sql is the name of the file where the backup will be saved.

If you want to backup all of the databases on a MySQL server, you can use the –all-databases flag:

```
$ mysqldump -u username -p --all-databases > all_databases_backup.sql
```

The backup file created by mysqldump can be restored using the MySQL command-line client:

```
$ mysql -u username -p dbname < dbname_backup.sql
```

This command will restore the database from the backup file into a database named dbname.

Backup with MySQL Enterprise Backup:

MySQL Enterprise Backup is a commercial tool that provides more advanced backup and restore capabilities than mysqldump. It supports incremental backups, partial backups, and point-in-time recovery.

To perform a backup using MySQL Enterprise Backup, you first need to install the tool on your server. Once installed, you can use the mysqlbackup command-line tool to create a backup:

```
$ mysqlbackup --login-path=backup --backup-dir=/backups backup
```

This command will create a full backup of all of the databases on the server and store it in the /backups directory.

To restore a backup created with MySQL Enterprise Backup, use the
mysqlbackup command-line tool:

```
$ mysqlbackup --login-path=restore --backup-dir=/backups copy-back
```

This command will restore the backup located in the /backups directory to the MySQL server.

Replication:

MySQL replication can also be used as a backup strategy. Replication
involves copying the data from one MySQL server (the master) to
another MySQL server (the slave). The slave server can be used for
read queries, backups, or failover scenarios.

To set up replication, you connect the slave server to the master server
and configure the necessary replication settings. The master server
will then automatically replicate changes to the slave server.

To use replication as a backup strategy, you can stop the replication,
take a backup of the slave server, and then restart the replication.
This ensures that the backup is consistent with the state of the slave
server.

Conclusion In conclusion, MySQL provides several options for performing backups and restoration of databases, including mysqldump,
MySQL Enterprise Backup, and replication. Each method has its advantages and disadvantages, and you should choose the method that
best suits your needs and requirements.

3.12   How do you use the MySQL LOAD DATA INFILE statement, and when is it beneficial to use?

The 'LOAD DATA INFILE' is a MySQL statement used to import
data from a file into a table. It allows for faster and more efficient
importing of data when compared to other methods such as using IN-
SERT statements. The syntax of the 'LOAD DATA INFILE' statement is as follows:

```
LOAD DATA INFILE 'path/to/file'
INTO TABLE table_name
FIELDS TERMINATED BY ','
ENCLOSED BY '"'
LINES TERMINATED BY 'n'
IGNORE 1 ROWS;
```

Let's break down the syntax:

- 'LOAD DATA INFILE': This is the statement used to indicate that data is being loaded from an external file into the MySQL database.

- ''path/to/file'': This is the path to the file where the data is located.

- 'INTO TABLE table_name': This is the name of the table into which the data will be imported.

- 'FIELDS TERMINATED BY ','': This specifies the character that separates the fields in the data file. In this case, the fields are separated by commas.

- 'ENCLOSED BY '"'': This specifies the character that encloses each field. In this case, the fields are enclosed by double quotes.

- 'LINES TERMINATED BY 'n'': This specifies the character that separates each line of data in the file. In this case, the lines are separated by a newline character.

- 'IGNORE 1 ROWS': This specifies that the first row of the file should be ignored, as it likely contains column headers or other information that is not data.

Apart from the above parameters, there are several other optional parameters that can be used, such as 'IGNORE', 'SET', 'CHARACTER SET', etc.

It is beneficial to use 'LOAD DATA INFILE' when importing large amounts of data into a MySQL database. Inserting data row by row using the 'INSERT' statement can be slow and time-consuming. In contrast, using 'LOAD DATA INFILE' can significantly reduce the time it takes to import large datasets. Additionally, this statement can handle a wide variety of file formats, such as CSV, TSV, and others.

However, there are some potential drawbacks to using 'LOAD DATA INFILE'. One issue can be with data integrity, as the file being imported may contain incorrect or invalid information. It's also important to ensure that the file is properly formatted and that the appropriate delimiter and encoding options are specified.

Overall, the 'LOAD DATA INFILE' statement is a great tool for efficient data importation in MySQL databases. Using this statement can save time and improve the speed of data importing.

3.13   Can you explain the concept of indexing, and what are the differences between a unique index and a full-text index in MySQL?

In MySQL, indexing refers to the process of creating an efficient data structure that enables faster searching, filtering, and sorting of data in a database table. Indexing allows MySQL to avoid scanning the entire table to find matching records, which can greatly improve query performance.

There are different types of indexes in MySQL, and two of the most common ones are unique indexes and full-text indexes.

A unique index is an index that enforces uniqueness on a column or a set of columns. It allows the database to ensure that no two rows in the same table have the same value in the indexed column(s). This type of index is useful when you want to enforce data consistency and prevent duplicate values in a column.

For example, let's say you have a table of users with the following columns: 'id', 'email', and 'name'. If you want to ensure that no two users have the same email address, you can create a unique index on the 'email' column:

```
CREATE UNIQUE INDEX email_unique_idx ON users (email);
```

Now, if you try to insert a new user with an email address that already exists in the table, MySQL will throw an error and prevent the insertion.

A full-text index, on the other hand, is an index that enables full-text search on one or more columns that contain text data, such as 'VARCHAR', 'TEXT', or 'BLOB'. Full-text search is a powerful feature that allows you to search for words or phrases within a text column, even if the words/phrases are not exact matches.

For example, let's say you have a blog with a 'posts' table that has a 'content' column storing the blog post content. You can create a full-text index on the content column to enable full-text search:

```
CREATE FULLTEXT INDEX content_fulltext_idx ON posts (content);
```

Now, you can search for posts that contain a given word or phrase using the 'MATCH' and 'AGAINST' keywords in a 'SELECT' statement:

```
SELECT * FROM posts WHERE MATCH (content) AGAINST ('cat video');
```

This query will return all posts that contain the words "cat" and "video", even if they're not next to each other or are in a different order.

To sum up, a unique index enforces uniqueness on a column or set of columns to prevent duplicates, while a full-text index enables full-text search on a text column to find words or phrases within the text.

3.14 How do you use the ALTER TABLE statement to modify an existing table's structure?

ALTER TABLE statement is used to modify the structure of an existing table in MySQL. We can use it to add, modify or delete columns, add or remove indexes, rename a table, and many more.

The syntax of the ALTER TABLE statement is as follows:

```
ALTER TABLE table_name action;
```

Here, 'table_name' is the name of the table that we want to modify and 'action' is the modification we want to make to the table.

Some of the most common modifications that can be made using ALTER TABLE are:

1. Adding a Column: We can use the 'ADD' keyword to add a new column to the table.

```
ALTER TABLE table_name ADD column_name column_definition;
```

Here, 'column_name' is the name of the column to be added and 'column_definition' specifies the data type and other properties of the column.

Example:

Suppose we have a table named 'students' with columns 'id', 'name', and 'age'. Now, we want to add a new column named 'email' to the table. The ALTER TABLE statement for this would be:

```
ALTER TABLE students ADD email VARCHAR(100);
```

2. Modifying a Column: We can use the 'MODIFY' keyword to modify the definition of an existing column.

```
ALTER TABLE table_name MODIFY column_name new_column_definition;
```

Here, 'column_name' is the name of the column to be modified and 'new_column_definition' specifies the new data type and other properties of the column.

Example:

Suppose we have a table named 'students' with a column 'age' of data type 'INT'. Now, we want to modify the data type of the column to 'SMALLINT'. The ALTER TABLE statement for this would be:

```
ALTER TABLE students MODIFY age SMALLINT;
```

3. Removing a Column: We can use the 'DROP' keyword to remove an existing column from the table.

```
ALTER TABLE table_name DROP column_name;
```

Here, 'column_name' is the name of the column to be removed.

Example:

Suppose we have a table named 'students' with columns 'id', 'name', 'age', and 'email'. Now, we want to remove the column named 'email' from the table. The ALTER TABLE statement for this would be:

```
ALTER TABLE students DROP email;
```

4. Renaming a Table: We can use the 'RENAME' keyword to rename an existing table.

```
ALTER TABLE old_table_name RENAME TO new_table_name;
```

Here, 'old_table_name' is the current name of the table and 'new_table_name' is the new name.

Example:

Suppose we have a table named 'students'. Now, we want to rename the table to 'classroom'. The ALTER TABLE statement for this would be:

```
ALTER TABLE students RENAME TO classroom;
```

These are some of the most common modifications that can be made using ALTER TABLE statement. However, there are many other modifications that can be made as well, such as adding or removing indexes, setting default values, and more.

3.15 What is the difference between a self-join and a cross join in MySQL?

In MySQL, self-join and cross join are two different types of joins used to combine data from two or more tables.

A self-join is a join in which a table is joined with itself. It is used when we want to combine rows from the same table based on some condition. In other words, it is a way of joining a table with itself. Self-joins are useful when we have a table that contains hierarchical data, such as an organization chart, where each row contains a reference to a parent row in the same table.

For example, suppose we have a table named employees with columns EmployeeId, EmployeeName, and ManagerId. The ManagerId col-

umn contains the EmployeeId of the employee's manager. To find
the name of the manager of each employee, we can use a self-join as
follows:

```
SELECT e.EmployeeName, m.EmployeeName as ManagerName
FROM employees e
JOIN employees m ON e.ManagerId = m.EmployeeId;
```

Here, we are joining the employees table with itself using the ManagerId and EmployeeId columns.

On the other hand, a cross join is used to combine all possible rows
from two or more tables. It is also known as a Cartesian product because it generates a result set that contains all possible combinations
of rows from the participating tables. In other words, it produces the
cross product of the two tables.

For example, suppose we have two tables named colors and sizes,
which contain the following data:

colors table:

```
| color |
|-------|
| red   |
| green |
| blue  |
```

sizes table:

```
| size |
|------|
| S    |
| M    |
| L    |
```

To generate a result set that contains all possible combinations of
colors and sizes, we can use a cross join as follows:

```
SELECT * FROM colors CROSS JOIN sizes;
```

The result of this query will be a table with all possible combinations
of rows from the colors and sizes tables:

```
| color | size |
|-------|------|
| red   | S    |
| red   | M    |
| red   | L    |
| green | S    |
```

```
| green | M |
| green | L |
| blue  | S |
| blue  | M |
| blue  | L |
```

In summary, the main difference between a self-join and a cross join is that a self-join is used to join a table with itself, while a cross join is used to generate a Cartesian product of two or more tables.

3.16 How do you use the CONCAT, CONCAT_WS, and SUBSTRING functions in MySQL?

In MySQL, the CONCAT, CONCAT_WS, and SUBSTRING functions are used for string manipulation. Here's an explanation of each function with some examples:

1. **CONCAT function:** The 'CONCAT' function is used to concatenate two or more strings into a single string. It takes one or more string arguments and returns a string.

Syntax:

```
CONCAT(string1, string2, ...)
```

Example:

```
SELECT CONCAT('Hello', '␣', 'World');
```

Output:

```
'Hello␣World'
```

2. **CONCAT_WS function:** The 'CONCAT_WS' function is used to concatenate strings with a separator. It takes a separator and two or more string arguments and returns a string with the separator between each of the strings.

Syntax:

```
CONCAT_WS(separator, string1, string2, ...)
```

Example:

```
SELECT CONCAT_WS(',', 'John', 'Doe', '25', 'Male');
```

Output:

```
'John,Doe,25,Male'
```

3. **SUBSTRING function:** The 'SUBSTRING' function is used to extract a substring from a string. It takes a string argument and two integer arguments that represent the starting position and the length of the substring.

Syntax:

```
SUBSTRING(string, start, length)
```

Example:

```
SELECT SUBSTRING('Hello␣World', 7, 5);
```

Output:

```
'World'
```

These functions are useful for manipulating strings in MySQL, whether you need to join strings together, add separators between strings, or extract a substring from a larger string.

3.17 What is an upsert operation, and how do you perform it using the IN-SERT ... ON DUPLICATE KEY UP-DATE statement in MySQL?

An upsert operation, also known as a merge operation, combines insert and update operations into a single statement. An upsert opera-

tion is used when you want to insert a row into a table if it does not
exist, or perform an update on the row if it already exists.

In MySQL, you can perform an upsert operation using the 'INSERT ...
ON DUPLICATE KEY UPDATE' statement. This statement works
by specifying the columns to be inserted, followed by the keyword
'VALUES', which contains the values to be inserted. If there is a
conflict with an existing row, the 'ON DUPLICATE KEY UPDATE'
clause is executed, updating the existing row.

Here is an example of using the 'INSERT ... ON DUPLICATE KEY
UPDATE' statement to perform an upsert operation in MySQL:

Suppose we have a table named 'users' with columns 'id', 'name',
and 'email'. We want to insert a new user record if the 'id' does not
exist in the table or update the 'name' and 'email' columns if the 'id'
already exists.

```
INSERT INTO users (id, name, email)
VALUES (1, 'John Smith', 'john.smith@example.com')
ON DUPLICATE KEY UPDATE
    name = VALUES(name),
    email = VALUES(email);
```

In this statement, we first specify the columns to be inserted ('id',
'name', and 'email') followed by the 'VALUES' keyword, which contains the values to be inserted ('1', ''John Smith'', and ''john.smith@ex-
ample.com'').

If the 'id' already exists in the 'users' table, the 'ON DUPLICATE
KEY UPDATE' clause is executed, updating the 'name' and 'email'
columns with the values specified in the 'VALUES' clause. The 'VAL-
UES()' function is used to reference the values originally intended to
be inserted.

Note that for this upsert operation to work, the 'id' column must be
defined as a unique key or primary key in the 'users' table.

3.18 What is the MySQL EXPLAIN statement, and how does it help in optimizing queries?

The MySQL EXPLAIN statement is a tool that helps in optimizing queries by providing critical information about how MySQL executes the query. It returns the execution plan of a SELECT, DELETE, INSERT, or UPDATE statement.

When you execute an EXPLAIN statement for a query, MySQL displays information on how it intends to execute the query. Specifically, it shows how it will access and combine rows in the selected tables. It also reveals whether MySQL can optimize the query, for example by using an index to access rows or by avoiding sorting operations, which could significantly speed up query execution.

The syntax for the EXPLAIN statement in MySQL is as follows:

```
EXPLAIN SELECT select_list FROM table_list [WHERE where_condition] [GROUP BY
    col_list] [ORDER BY col_list] [LIMIT rows]
```

The output of the EXPLAIN statement contains the following columns:

- id: A sequential number that represents the order in which MySQL executes the query.

- select_type: The type of SELECT statement that MySQL uses to execute the query. Examples include SIMPLE, SUBQUERY, UNION, and DERIVED.

- table: The name of the table that MySQL accesses to retrieve data. If a query involves multiple tables, the table listed first is typically the one that MySQL accesses first.

- partitions: If the table is partitioned, this column will show the partitioning type and any partitioning expressions used.

- type: The type of access method that MySQL uses to access data from the table. Examples include ALL, UNIQUE_INDEX, RANGE, and REF.

- possible_keys: The list of indexes that MySQL can use to execute the query.

- key: The index that MySQL selects to execute the query. If the value of this column is NULL, it means that MySQL cannot use any index to execute the query.

- key_len: The length of the index that MySQL uses to execute the query.

- ref: The columns or constants that MySQL compares to the index.

- rows: The number of rows that MySQL examines to execute the query.

- filtered: The percentage of rows that MySQL filters out using the WHERE clause or other conditions.

- Extra: Additional information about how MySQL executes the query, such as whether it uses a temporary table or a file sort.

By studying the output of the EXPLAIN statement, you can identify potential performance bottlenecks and optimize the query accordingly. For example, you can use the information from the output to make sure that you have the appropriate indexes in place, or to identify whether MySQL performs a full table scan rather than using an index.

In summary, the MySQL EXPLAIN statement provides valuable information about how MySQL executes a query, which can help you identify performance bottlenecks and optimize your queries for maximum efficiency.

3.19 What are the differences between the various types of MySQL locks: shared locks, exclusive locks, and intention locks?

MySQL Locks are used to manage concurrent accesses to the same data, ensuring data consistency and preventing race conditions. MySQL supports several types of locks, including shared locks, exclusive locks, and intention locks.

Shared Locks: Shared locks (also known as Read lock) allow multiple sessions to read a specific resource simultaneously, while preventing any of them from modifying the resource. A shared lock does not conflict with another shared lock, but it conflicts with an exclusive lock.

To acquire a shared lock on a resource, you can use the 'SELECT

... LOCK IN SHARE MODE' statement. For example, the following query acquires a shared lock on the 'employees' table:

```
SELECT * FROM employees LOCK IN SHARE MODE;
```

Exclusive Locks: Exclusive locks (also known as Write lock) allow only one session to modify a specific resource, while preventing any other sessions from reading or modifying the resource. An exclusive lock conflicts with any shared or exclusive locks.

To acquire an exclusive lock on a resource, you can use the 'SELECT ... FOR UPDATE' statement. For example, the following query acquires an exclusive lock on the 'employees' table:

```
SELECT * FROM employees WHERE id = 1 FOR UPDATE;
```

Intention Locks: Intention locks are used to indicate the intention to acquire a shared or exclusive lock on a resource at a higher level of granularity. These locks do not prevent other sessions from acquiring the same intention lock.

There are two types of intention locks: 'INTENTION SHARED' (IS) and 'INTENTION EXCLUSIVE' (IX). An 'IS' lock indicates the intention to acquire a shared lock on a resource at a lower level of granularity, while an 'IX' lock indicates the intention to acquire an exclusive lock on a resource at a lower level of granularity.

For example, to acquire an intention lock on a table, you can use the 'LOCK TABLES' statement:

```
LOCK TABLES employees INTENTION SHARED;
```

This statement acquires an 'IS' lock on the 'employees' table, indicating the intention to acquire a shared lock on the table at a lower level of granularity.

In summary, shared locks allow multiple sessions to read a specific resource, exclusive locks allow only one session to modify a specific resource, and intention locks indicate the intention to acquire a lock on a resource at a lower level of granularity. It's important to choose the right type of lock depending on the use case to ensure proper concurrency control, prevent deadlocks and optimize performance.

3.20 Can you explain the difference between pessimistic and optimistic concurrency control in MySQL?

Concurrency control is the process used to manage the access and modification of shared resources among multiple users in a database system. Optimistic and pessimistic concurrency control are two approaches used to manage concurrent transactions in a database.

Pessimistic concurrency control (PCC) is based on the assumption that conflicts are likely to occur during concurrent transactions. Therefore, PCC requires that transactions lock resources in the database (e.g., tables, rows, or columns) during their processing time to avoid conflicts. This locking mechanism prevents other transactions from accessing or modifying locked resources, which may result in blocking and deadlocks. PCC is suitable for database systems with high contention workloads, where transactions often require exclusive access to the same resource(s) and are therefore prone to conflicts.

Here is an example of a pessimistic concurrency control approach in MySQL using the 'SELECT ... FOR UPDATE' statement. The 'SELECT ... FOR UPDATE' statement is used to retrieve rows from a table while locking them to prevent other transactions from accessing them until the transaction that holds the lock completes.

```
START TRANSACTION;
SELECT * FROM accounts WHERE id = 1 FOR UPDATE;
UPDATE accounts SET balance = balance + 100 WHERE id = 1;
COMMIT;
```

Optimistic concurrency control (OCC) is based on the assumption that conflicts between transactions are infrequent. Therefore, OCC does not require locks to manage concurrency. Instead, each transaction reads the current state of a resource and applies changes to it in memory, without updating the resource in the database. Before committing changes, the transaction verifies that the resource's state has not changed since the transaction started. If the state has changed, the transaction rolls back and can retry the operation. OCC is suitable for database systems with low contention workloads, where conflicts are less likely to occur.

Here is an example of optimistic concurrency control approach in

MySQL using the 'SELECT ... FOR UPDATE' syntax. In this example, '@version' variable holds the current value, and if the value is
the same at the time we execute the update query, then the row is
updated with a new value, and the version is incremented.

```
START TRANSACTION;
SELECT balance INTO @balance, version INTO @version FROM accounts WHERE id =
    1;
SET @balance = @balance + 100, @version = @version + 1;
UPDATE accounts SET balance = @balance, version = @version WHERE id = 1 AND
    version = @version - 1;
IF ROW_COUNT() = 0 THEN
    ROLLBACK;
ELSE
    COMMIT;
END IF;
```

In summary, Pessimistic concurrency control uses locks to prevent
conflicts between transactions, while optimistic concurrency control
uses in-memory processing without locks and checks for conflicts after
the transaction is complete. The choice between the two approaches
depends on the workload and requirements of the database system.

Chapter 4

Advanced

4.1 What is the purpose of MySQL's query optimizer, and how does it work?

MySQL's query optimizer is responsible for finding the most efficient way to execute a query. Its main purpose is to examine the available indexes, statistics, and other relevant properties of the tables being queried to generate an execution plan that minimizes response time and maximizes resource utilization.

To achieve this goal, the optimizer uses a variety of techniques and algorithms, including:

1. Cost-based optimization: This technique assigns a cost to each possible execution plan and selects the plan with the lowest cost. The cost is typically calculated based on factors such as the number of disk reads, CPU cycles, and network traffic involved in executing the plan.

2. Join order optimization: This technique determines the most efficient order in which to join the tables in a query. The optimizer considers factors such as the size of the tables, the available indexes, and the join conditions to determine the join order that will result in the lowest cost.

3. Index selection: The optimizer chooses the most appropriate index
to use for each table based on the query's filter conditions and join
predicates. It considers factors such as the selectivity of the index,
its cardinality, and its clustering factor.

4. Query transformation: Sometimes the optimizer can transform a
query to a more efficient form. For example, it can replace a subquery
with a join.

To illustrate how the optimizer works, consider the following query:

```
SELECT *
FROM customers
JOIN orders ON customers.id = orders.customer_id
WHERE customers.state = 'CA';
```

The optimizer would follow a process similar to the following:

1. Determine the join order. In this case, it would likely join the
customers table with the orders table.

2. Choose the most appropriate index for each table. Suppose the
customers table has an index on the state column and the orders table
has an index on the customer_id column. The optimizer would likely
use the index on the customers.state column to filter the rows from
the customers table and then use the index on the orders.customer_id
column to join the two tables.

3. Evaluate the cost of the execution plan. The optimizer would
estimate the cost of using the chosen join order and index selection,
taking into account factors such as the table sizes and the selectivity
of the indexes.

4. Choose the plan with the lowest cost. The optimizer would compare the costs of all possible execution plans and select the one with
the lowest cost.

Overall, the query optimizer is a critical component of MySQL's performance optimization, and its ability to select the most efficient execution plan can make a significant difference in query response time
and overall database performance.

4.2 How do you handle large datasets and improve query performance using partitioning in MySQL?

Partitioning is a technique used in MySQL to partition large tables into smaller, more manageable pieces. By doing so, we can improve query performance as well as make it easier to manage and maintain the database.

There are several methods of partitioning available in MySQL, including:

1. Range partitioning: Data is partitioned based on a specified range of values, such as partitioning orders by date.

2. Hash partitioning: Data is partitioned based on a hash value, such as partitioning user data based on their ID.

3. Key partitioning: Similar to hash partitioning, but the partitioning is done based on a specific key.

To demonstrate how partitioning can be used to improve query performance, consider the following example. Let's say we have a table containing sales data for a large online store. This table contains millions of rows of data, and we want to run a query to find the total sales for a particular month. Without partitioning, this query might take a considerable amount of time to run, especially if the table is not indexed properly.

To improve query performance, we can partition the sales table by date using range partitioning. This allows us to easily isolate data for a particular month, making queries faster and more efficient. For example, we could partition the table into monthly partitions, with each partition containing data for a specific month.

Here is an example of how to create a partitioned table in MySQL:

```
CREATE TABLE sales (
    sales_id INT NOT NULL,
    sales_date DATE NOT NULL,
    sales_total DECIMAL(10,2) NOT NULL
)
PARTITION BY RANGE(YEAR(sales_date)*100 + MONTH(sales_date)) (
    PARTITION p0 VALUES LESS THAN (20180101),
    PARTITION p1 VALUES LESS THAN (20180201),
    PARTITION p2 VALUES LESS THAN (20180301),
```

```
...
PARTITION p12 VALUES LESS THAN (20190101)
);
```

In the above example, we are partitioning the sales table by month using the 'RANGE' option. Each partition is defined using a 'VALUES LESS THAN' clause, which specifies the upper bound for each partition.

Once the table is partitioned, we can run queries that only access the partitions we're interested in, which can significantly improve performance. For example, to find the total sales for January 2018, we could run the following query:

```
SELECT SUM(sales_total) FROM sales PARTITION(p0);
```

This query only accesses the partition for January 2018, making it much faster than a query that would scan the entire table.

In conclusion, using partitioning in MySQL can greatly improve query performance for large datasets. By partitioning data based on specific criteria, we can easily isolate and query subsets of the data without having to scan the entire table.

4.3   What are the different types of replication in MySQL, and how do they work?

MySQL Replication is the process of copying data from one database to another in a master-slave architecture. It is a powerful feature that allows data to be distributed across multiple MySQL servers for high availability or load balancing. There are different types of MySQL Replication, which are:

1. Statement-based replication (SBR): Statement-based replication (SBR) is the default replication mode in MySQL. In SBR, the SQL statements executed on the master server are stored in the binary log, which is then used to replay the same statements on the slave server(s) to replicate the data. SBR can be used for simple replication setups and is generally faster than row-based replication but

can lead to issues with non-deterministic statements. For Example, the statement "INSERT INTO table_name (sometext) VALUES (DATE_FORMAT(NOW(),'

2. Row-based replication (RBR): Row-based replication (RBR) replicates the actual rows changed on the master server to the slave servers. In this mode, the log events for the row change are actually written to the binary log. As a result, RBR provides a more accurate duplication of the data from the master to the slave, often resulting in better data integrity. RBR is ideal for databases that use non-deterministic functions but can lead to increased network traffic and storage requirements on the slave server.

3. Mixed-based replication: Mixed-based replication is a mode in which MySQL uses both statement-based and row-based replication methods, depending on the type of SQL statement being executed. In this mode, deterministic statements, such as INSERT or UPDATE statements that do not use non-deterministic functions, are logged using the statement-based method, whereas non-deterministic statements, such as those that use the NOW () function, are logged using row-based replication.

Each of these replication types has its own benefits and drawbacks. Choosing the right replication mode depends on the specific needs of the database setup. In general, SBR is faster and requires less storage, but can have issues with non-deterministic functions. RBR provides better data integrity, but can be slower and more storage-intensive. Mixed-based replication, as the name suggests, offers the best of both worlds, but requires careful configuration to balance the benefits against the drawbacks.

4.4 How do you use the MySQL Performance Schema to analyze and improve query performance?

MySQL Performance Schema is a powerful tool that can be used to analyze and optimize query performance. Here are some steps to effectively use Performance Schema for this purpose:

1. Enable Performance Schema: Performance Schema is disabled by
default in MySQL. To enable it, you need to add the following line
to your MySQL configuration file:

```
performance_schema=ON
```

2. Identify slow queries: Once Performance Schema is enabled, you
can use the 'performance_schema' database to identify slow queries.
The 'performance_schema' database contains several tables that provide information on query performance, including the 'events_state-
ments_summary_by_digest' table which summarizes the performance
statistics for each query digest. To view the slowest queries, you can
run the following query:

```
SELECT * FROM performance_schema.events_statements_summary_by_digest ORDER BY
    SUM_TIMER_WAIT DESC LIMIT 10;
```

This query will show the top 10 slowest queries, ordered by their total
wait time across all executions.

3. Analyze query execution plan: To optimize query performance, it
is important to understand how the query is executed. Performance
Schema provides a table called 'events_stages_summary_by_digest'
which provides information on the query execution plan. This table
contains information on each stage of query execution, including the
number of executions, total and average wait time, and the percentage
of time spent in each stage. To view the execution plan for a specific
query, you can run the following query:

```
SELECT * FROM performance_schema.events_stages_summary_by_digest WHERE digest
    = 'QUERY_DIGEST';
```

Replace 'QUERY_DIGEST' with the digest value of the query you
want to analyze.

4. Identify resource-intensive queries: Performance Schema provides
several tables that can help you identify resource-intensive queries.
For example, the 'events_waits_summary_global_by_event_name'
table summarizes wait events by event name, which can help you
identify queries that are causing high CPU or I/O usage. You can
use the following query to view the top 10 wait events by total wait
time:

```
SELECT * FROM performance_schema.events_waits_summary_global_by_event_name
    ORDER BY SUM_TIMER_WAIT DESC LIMIT 10;
```

5. Optimize queries: Once you have identified slow and resource-intensive queries, you can take steps to optimize them. This may involve adding indexes, rewriting the query, or optimizing the database schema. You can use the 'EXPLAIN' statement to analyze query execution plans and identify areas for optimization. Additionally, you can use profiling tools such as 'pt-query-digest' or 'mysqlslap' to simulate query loads and test performance improvements.

In summary, MySQL Performance Schema is a powerful tool that can be used to analyze and optimize query performance. By identifying slow and resource-intensive queries, analyzing query execution plans, and optimizing queries and database schema, you can significantly improve the performance of your MySQL database.

4.5 Can you explain the concept of foreign key constraints with cascading actions like CASCADE, SET NULL, and SET DEFAULT in MySQL?

In MySQL, a foreign key constraint is a key that refers to the primary key of another table. This constraint ensures that the data being inserted or updated in a table is consistent with the related table. Foreign key constraints can also be used to automatically perform cascading actions when a primary key is updated or deleted.

There are three types of cascading actions in MySQL:

1. CASCADE: When a record is updated or deleted from the primary key table, the changes are cascaded to the foreign key table. For example, if a record in the primary key table is deleted, all related records in the foreign key table are also deleted.

2. SET NULL: When a record is updated or deleted from the primary key table, the corresponding value in the foreign key table is set to NULL. For example, if a record in the primary key table is deleted, the corresponding foreign key value in the related table is set to NULL.

3. SET DEFAULT: When a record is updated or deleted from the

primary key table, the corresponding value in the foreign key table is set to its default value. The default value must be defined when the foreign key constraint is created.

Here's an example of how to create a foreign key constraint with a cascading action in MySQL:

```
CREATE TABLE orders (
  order_id INT,
  customer_id INT,
  order_date DATE,
  PRIMARY KEY (order_id)
);

CREATE TABLE customers (
  customer_id INT,
  customer_name VARCHAR(20),
  PRIMARY KEY (customer_id),
  FOREIGN KEY (customer_id)
    REFERENCES orders(customer_id)
    ON DELETE CASCADE
    ON UPDATE CASCADE
);
```

In this example, the 'customers' table has a foreign key constraint that refers to the 'customer_id' column of the 'orders' table. The 'CASCADE' action is specified for both the 'ON DELETE' and 'ON UPDATE' options, which means that any changes made to the 'customer_id' column of the 'orders' table will be cascaded to the 'customer_id' column of the 'customers' table.

4.6   What is a deadlock in MySQL, and how can you prevent and resolve deadlocks?

A deadlock occurs in MySQL when two or more transactions are waiting for one another to release a lock on a resource that they need. This results in a deadlock situation, where none of the transactions can proceed further, and the database essentially hangs. MySQL uses lock-based concurrency control to manage concurrent access to data. These locks can be at the table-level or at a row-level.

There are several ways to prevent and resolve deadlocks in MySQL.

1. The simplest way to prevent deadlocks is to ensure that all trans-

actions acquire their locks in the same order. This can prevent situations where transactions are waiting for resources that are held by other transactions.

2. Another approach is to use shorter transactions. By breaking up long transactions into smaller units, you reduce the chances of a deadlock occurring.

3. You can also optimize the queries that are being executed in the transactions. Queries that are poorly optimized can take longer to execute, which increases the likelihood of a deadlock occurring.

4. InnoDB, the default storage engine for MySQL, provides some tools for detecting and resolving deadlocks. You can use the 'SHOW ENGINE INNODB STATUS' command to get a detailed report of all the transactions that are currently running, as well as information on any deadlocks that have occurred.

5. If a deadlock occurs, one way to resolve it is to kill one of the transactions. MySQL will automatically roll back any changes made by the killed transaction, which will free up the resources that the other transaction was waiting for.

6. Another approach is to use timeouts. By setting a timeout on transactions, you can ensure that they don't run for too long, which reduces the likelihood of a deadlock occurring.

7. Finally, you can use indexing to improve the performance of your queries. By creating indexes on the columns that are frequently used in your queries, you can speed up their execution, which reduces the amount of time that transactions need to hold locks on resources.

In conclusion, deadlocks can be prevented and resolved in MySQL by optimizing queries, using shorter transactions, setting timeouts, using indexing, and using tools provided by InnoDB engine such as 'SHOW ENGINE INNODB STATUS' command.

4.7 How do you use MySQL's event scheduler to automate tasks in the database?

MySQL's Event Scheduler is a tool that allows you to automate tasks within the database without having to rely on external applications or scripts. With this tool, you can schedule tasks to run on a regular basis, or at specific times, which can help you to keep your database running smoothly and efficiently.

To use MySQL's Event Scheduler, you need to follow these steps:

1. Enable the Event Scheduler: The event scheduler is disabled by default in MySQL, so you need to enable it before you can create any events. You can do this by setting the 'event_scheduler' system variable to 'ON'. This can be done at runtime using the 'SET' command:

```
SET GLOBAL event_scheduler = ON;
```

Alternatively, you can enable it permanently by adding the following line to your MySQL configuration file:

```
event_scheduler = ON
```

2. Create an Event: Once the event scheduler is enabled, you can create events using the 'CREATE EVENT' command. This command allows you to specify a name for the event, as well as the schedule and the SQL statement that should be executed when the event runs. Here's an example of a simple event that runs every hour:

```
CREATE EVENT my_event
ON SCHEDULE EVERY 1 HOUR
DO
   UPDATE my_table SET my_column = my_column + 1;
```

This event will run every hour and update the 'my_table' table by incrementing the value in the 'my_column' column by 1.

3. Manage Events: Once you have created an event, you can manage it using the 'ALTER EVENT' and 'DROP EVENT' commands. The 'ALTER EVENT' command allows you to modify the schedule or the SQL statement that is executed when the event runs. The 'DROP EVENT' command allows you to delete an event.

Here's an example of modifying the schedule of an event:

```
ALTER EVENT my_event
ON SCHEDULE EVERY 2 HOURS;
```

This will change the schedule of the 'my_event' event to run every 2 hours instead of every hour.

And here's an example of deleting an event:

```
DROP EVENT my_event;
```

This will delete the 'my_event' event.

In conclusion, MySQL's Event Scheduler is a powerful tool that can help you to automate tasks within your database. By following these steps, you can enable the event scheduler, create events, and manage them as needed.

4.8 What are the best practices for securing a MySQL database?

Securing a MySQL database is critical to protect sensitive data from unauthorized access, disclosure, modification, destruction, and other possible threats. There are several best practices that can help to secure a MySQL database. Some of them are listed below:

1. Using Strong Authentication:

MySQL users should have strong passwords that are difficult to guess, contain a minimum of eight characters, and use a combination of letters, numbers, and symbols. Avoid using common passwords such as "password", "123456", etc., as they are easily guessable by attackers. Also, enable two-factor authentication (2FA) for additional security.

2. Limiting Access:

Limiting the access of MySQL server to only authorized users is important. Grant only the necessary privileges required for each user and avoid granting all privileges to root or other users. Additionally, ensure that MySQL is not accessible from the internet or any public network.

3. Encrypting Data:

Sensitive data that is being stored in a MySQL database should be encrypted. MySQL provides several data encryption options such as AES_ENCRYPT, AES_DECRYPT, and SSL encryption. Encryption can ensure that even if the data is stolen, it will not be usable without the decryption key.

4. Updating and Patching:

MySQL database software should be updated and patched regularly to fix known vulnerabilities and security issues. Over time, security risks emerge and new versions of MySQL can have improved security features.

5. Enabling Logging:

Enable logging to keep track of all database activities, such as logins, queries, and access attempts. This record can be used to detect unauthorized access and other security incidents.

6. Background Checks:

Perform background checks on all employees or subcontractors who will have access to the MySQL database. A security breach can also be the result of someone malicious inside the company. Access rights should be given only to those who require them to do their jobs.

7. Firewall Configuration:

MySQL must be configured to either allow incoming connections from trusted addresses only or to deny all incoming connections. A firewall can be used to block unauthorized access to the database.

In conclusion, securing a MySQL database should be taken very seriously by any organization that stores sensitive data. The list above is a good starting point, but must be adapted to each specific situation to create a database that is both secure and functional.

4.9 How do you troubleshoot and resolve MySQL performance issues related to slow queries or high CPU/memory usage?

When dealing with MySQL performance issues related to slow queries or high CPU/memory usage, there are several steps you can take in order to troubleshoot and resolve the problem. Here are some of the key steps you can follow:

1. Identify the problem queries: The first step in troubleshooting any MySQL performance issue is to identify the specific queries that are causing the problem. You can use MySQL's built-in performance monitoring tools (such as the slow query log) or third-party profiling tools (such as the Percona Toolkit) to identify slow queries and analyze their performance characteristics.

2. Optimize the queries: Once you have identified the slow queries, the next step is to optimize them. This may involve changing the query structure, adding or removing indexes, or rewriting the queries altogether. There are several techniques and best practices for query optimization, such as using efficient WHERE clauses, avoiding unnecessary joins or subqueries, and limiting the amount of data returned by the queries.

3. Optimize the MySQL configuration: In addition to optimizing the queries themselves, you can also optimize the MySQL server configuration to improve performance. This may involve tweaking parameters such as the buffer sizes, thread concurrency, and query cache settings. There are many resources available online that can provide guidance on the best MySQL configuration settings for different types of workloads.

4. Scale up or out: If query optimization and configuration tuning do not provide sufficient performance improvements, you may need to consider scaling up or out your MySQL environment. Scaling up involves adding more resources (such as CPU, memory, or disk space) to the existing MySQL server, while scaling out involves adding additional servers to distribute the workload across a larger number of nodes. There are several tools available for managing MySQL clusters

and for conducting load balancing across multiple nodes.

5. Monitor ongoing performance: Once you have resolved the imme-
diate performance issue, it is important to continue monitoring the
MySQL server for ongoing performance issues. This can help you
identify potential problems early and take corrective action before
they have a major impact on the application. There are several monitoring tools and services available that can provide real-time insights
into the performance of your MySQL environment, such as MySQL
Enterprise Monitor and Grafana.

Here is an example of a slow query that uses inefficient JOIN and
WHERE clauses, and how you could optimize it:

```
SELECT *
FROM orders o
JOIN order_items oi ON o.id = oi.order_id
JOIN products p ON oi.product_id = p.id
WHERE p.category = 'Clothing' AND o.status = 'completed'
```

To optimize the query, you could rewrite it as follows:

```
SELECT *
FROM orders o
JOIN (
  SELECT order_id, product_id
  FROM order_items oi
  JOIN products p ON oi.product_id = p.id
  WHERE p.category = 'Clothing'
) oi ON o.id = oi.order_id
WHERE o.status = 'completed'
```

This query uses a subquery to filter the order_items table by product
category before joining it with the orders table, which can significantly
reduce the amount of data that needs to be processed.

4.10   How do you implement connection pooling in MySQL to improve performance?

Connection pooling is a technique that allows efficient database con-
nectivity from a web application. It maintains a cache of database
connections so that the connections can be reused when the application requests a database connection rather than opening a new

database connection for each request. This technique can improve the performance of the database significantly.

To implement connection pooling in MySQL, follow the steps below:

1. Download a JDBC driver that supports connection pooling. For example, the commons-dbcp2 library can be used.

2. Initialize the connection pool by creating an object of the connection pool configuration interface. This object can be created by setting the connection properties such as the JDBC driver, database URL, username, and password.

Configuring the Connection Pool

```
import java.sql.Connection;
import java.sql.SQLException;
import org.apache.commons.dbcp2.BasicDataSource;

public class ConnectionPool {
  private BasicDataSource connectionPool = new BasicDataSource();

  public ConnectionPool() {
    connectionPool.setDriverClassName("com.mysql.jdbc.Driver");
    connectionPool.setUrl("jdbc:mysql://localhost:3306/mydatabase");
    connectionPool.setUsername("root");
    connectionPool.setPassword("password");
  }

  public Connection getConnection() throws SQLException {
    return connectionPool.getConnection();
  }
}
```

In the above example, a connection pool is created using the BasicDataSource class provided by the commons-dbcp2 library. The connection properties are configured using the setDriverClassName, setUrl, setUsername, and setPassword methods.

3. Use the initialized connection pool to obtain and release connections for database operations.

Using the Connection Pool

```
import java.sql.Connection;
import java.sql.PreparedStatement;
import java.sql.SQLException;

public class EmployeeDAO {
  private ConnectionPool connectionPool = new ConnectionPool();

  public void save(Employee employee) throws SQLException {
    Connection connection = null;
    PreparedStatement statement = null;
```

```
    try {
      connection = connectionPool.getConnection();
      statement = connection.prepareStatement("INSERT␣INTO␣Employee␣VALUES
          (?,␣?,␣?)");
      statement.setInt(1, employee.getId());
      statement.setString(2, employee.getName());
      statement.setInt(3, employee.getAge());
      statement.executeUpdate();
    } finally {
      releaseResources(connection, statement);
    }
  }

  private void releaseResources(Connection connection, PreparedStatement
      statement) {
    try {
      if (statement != null) {
        statement.close();
      }
      if (connection != null) {
        connection.close();
      }
    } catch (SQLException e) {
      System.out.println("Error␣while␣closing␣resources" + e.getMessage());
    }
  }
}
```

In the above example, the connection pool is used to obtain a connection and a prepared statement is created to execute the SQL query. After the database operations are complete, the connection and statement objects are released back to the connection pool using the releaseResources method.

Connection pooling can help improve the performance of web applications where there are many users accessing the database simultaneously. By reusing existing database connections, the overhead of creating and destroying connections is eliminated, resulting in improved performance and reduced resource consumption.

4.11   What is the role of buffer pools in InnoDB storage engine, and how do they affect MySQL performance?

InnoDB storage engine is the default storage engine for MySQL. It is a transactional storage engine that uses a buffer pool to cache data in memory so that frequently accessed data can be served from memory rather than disk. This helps improve the performance of read operations, which is a common bottleneck in database systems.

The buffer pool is essentially a memory cache that InnoDB uses to store frequently accessed data. Whenever a query is executed, InnoDB checks if the required data is already present in the buffer pool. If the data is found, it is served from memory directly, otherwise, the necessary data is read from disk and stored in the buffer pool before being served to the query.

The size of the buffer pool is configurable and can be set using the 'innodb_buffer_pool_size' system variable. The recommended size of the buffer pool is typically around 70-80

The buffer pool is divided into pages, each of which is typically 16KB in size. The pages are organized in a LRU (Least Recently Used) algorithm, which means that the oldest and least frequently accessed pages are removed from the buffer pool to make space for new pages that need to be cached.

The buffer pool also plays an important role in write operations. Whenever a write operation is executed, InnoDB writes the changes to the buffer pool first and then to disk at a later time. This is known as write buffering and helps optimize disk I/O by reducing the number of times data needs to be written to disk.

The buffer pool can have a significant impact on MySQL performance. If the buffer pool is too small, MySQL may need to read data from disk frequently, which can slow down read operations. On the other hand, if the buffer pool is too large, it can lead to performance degradation due to excessive memory consumption.

In conclusion, the buffer pool is a critical component of InnoDB storage engine in MySQL. It provides an efficient mechanism for storing frequently accessed data in memory, and can significantly improve the performance of read operations. Properly configuring the buffer pool size is crucial for optimizing MySQL performance.

4.12   How do you use the FLUSH TA-BLES WITH READ LOCK statement in MySQL, and when is it necessary?

The 'FLUSH TABLES WITH READ LOCK' is a statement in MySQL that is used to acquire a global read lock on all tables in a database. This ensures that no other session can modify data in these tables, at least until the lock is released or the session acquiring the lock is terminated. In other words, the statement flushes all changes from the table cache to disk, and then prevents any further changes until it is released.

The 'FLUSH TABLES WITH READ LOCK' statement can be issued in two ways:

1. Within a transaction:

```
START TRANSACTION;
FLUSH TABLES WITH READ LOCK;
# ... perform some operations on the tables ...
COMMIT;
```

2. Outside a transaction:

```
FLUSH TABLES WITH READ LOCK;
# ... perform some operations on the tables ...
UNLOCK TABLES;
```

It is usually used by database administrators (DBAs) to perform backups or migrations on a running database server without disrupting the normal operations of the database. By acquiring a read lock, the DBA ensures that the data being backed up or migrated is consistent at the point in time when the lock is acquired. Moreover, since the lock prevents any writes to the database, it reduces the risk of data corruption during the backup or migration process.

It is important to note that while the 'FLUSH TABLES WITH READ LOCK' statement is in effect, no session can modify the tables until the lock is released. This might cause significant performance degradation, which means that this statement should be used with caution and only for short periods of time.

In summary, the 'FLUSH TABLES WITH READ LOCK' statement

is a powerful tool that is useful for ensuring consistency in a database and preventing data corruption during backups or migrations. However, it should be used with caution and only for short periods of time to avoid any negative impact on database performance.

4.13   How do you monitor and manage long-running queries in MySQL?

In MySQL, long-running queries can cause performance issues and slow down the database system. It is important to monitor and manage these queries to ensure optimal performance. Some ways to monitor and manage long-running queries in MySQL are:

1. Use the slow query log: MySQL has a built-in slow query log feature that records queries that take longer than a specified time to execute. By enabling this feature, you can identify slow queries and analyze them to optimize their performance. To enable the slow query log, add the following lines to your MySQL configuration file:

```
slow_query_log = 1
slow_query_log_file = /var/log/mysql/mysql-slow.log
long_query_time = 5
```

This configures MySQL to log queries that take longer than 5 seconds to execute to the specified log file.

2. Use the Performance Schema: The Performance Schema is a feature in MySQL that provides detailed information about database performance. It can be used to monitor queries and identify performance bottlenecks. You can use the Performance Schema to analyze long-running queries and find ways to optimize them.

3. Use tools like MySQL Enterprise Monitor and Query Analyzer: MySQL Enterprise Monitor is a monitoring tool that provides real-time monitoring of MySQL databases. It can be used to identify long-running queries and analyze their performance. MySQL Query Analyzer is a tool that can be used to analyze SQL statements and identify performance issues. It can be used to analyze long-running queries and optimize their performance.

4. Use EXPLAIN to analyze query execution plans: The EXPLAIN
statement can be used to analyze how MySQL executes a query. It
can be used to identify performance issues and optimize query performance. By analyzing the execution plan of a long-running query,
you can identify performance bottlenecks and optimize the query.

In summary, there are many ways to monitor and manage long-
running queries in MySQL. By using tools like the slow query log,
Performance Schema, MySQL Enterprise Monitor, Query Analyzer,
and EXPLAIN, you can identify and optimize long-running queries
to ensure optimal database performance.

4.14   What is the purpose of binary logs in MySQL, and how do they help in point-in-time recovery?

Binary logs in MySQL are used for recording all the changes that
are made to a database server. They are used for various purposes,
such as replication, point-in-time recovery, auditing, backup, and data
analysis. In this answer, we will focus on their role in point-in-time
recovery.

Point-in-time recovery is the process of restoring a database to a specific point in time, which is typically just before a critical event, such
as a system failure, data corruption, or human error. This is important for ensuring data integrity, business continuity, and regulatory
compliance.

Binary logs help in point-in-time recovery by providing a way to replay database changes from a specific point in time to another. This
is achieved by restoring an earlier backup of the database, and then
applying the binary logs that were generated after the backup was
taken until the desired point in time is reached. This process is called
roll-forward recovery.

To understand this process better, let us consider an example. Suppose we have a MySQL database with a table called 'users', which
has the following records:

```
+----+---------+------------+
| id | name    | email      |
+----+---------+------------+
| 1  | Alice   | alice@example.com|
| 2  | Bob     | bob@example.com|
| 3  | Charlie | charlie@example.com|
+----+---------+------------+
```

Suppose that at 12:00 PM, a user named David accidentally deleted the record for Alice, and we want to recover the database to the state just before that event. Here is how we can do it using binary logs:

1. First, we need to identify the timestamp of the last backup that was taken before the event. Suppose the backup was taken at 11:00 AM. 2. We restore the backup to a new server, which will have the same schema as the original server but will not have any of the changes made after 11:00 AM. 3. We then play the binary logs forward from 11:00 AM until just before the delete statement that caused the issue. To do this, we use the 'mysqlbinlog' utility to read the binary logs and filter the events that we want to apply. The command would look something like this:

```
mysqlbinlog --start-datetime='2021-07-01 11:00:00' --stop-datetime='
    2021-07-01 12:00:00' mysql-bin.000001 | mysql -h newserver -u root -p
```

This command will read the binary logs from 'mysql-bin.000001' between the timestamps of 11:00 AM and 12:00 PM and apply them to the new server. 4. Finally, we verify that the database has been recovered successfully and that the record for Alice is back in the 'users' table.

In summary, binary logs are essential for point-in-time recovery in MySQL as they provide a way to replay database changes from a specific point in time to another. This is critical for ensuring data integrity and business continuity in the event of a failure or error.

4.15   What are the differences between one-way and two-way SSL authentication in MySQL, and how do you configure them?

Secure Sockets Layer (SSL) is a protocol used to encrypt the communication between the client and the server, providing secure data transmission over a network. MySQL server can be configured with either one-way SSL authentication or two-way SSL authentication to establish secure connections.

One-way SSL authentication, also known as SSL client authentication, is a type of SSL authentication that only requires the client to authenticate the server. The server presents its SSL certificate to the client, and the client verifies the certificate's authenticity. If the certificate is trusted, the connection is established, and the communication between the client and the server is encrypted.

Two-way SSL authentication, also known as mutual SSL authentication, is a type of SSL authentication that requires both the client and the server to authenticate each other. The client presents its SSL certificate to the server, and the server verifies the certificate's authenticity. The server also presents its SSL certificate to the client, and the client verifies the certificate's authenticity. If both certificates are trusted, the connection is established, and the communication between the client and the server is encrypted.

To configure one-way SSL authentication in MySQL, you need to generate an SSL certificate for the server and configure MySQL to use it. Here are the steps to follow:

1. Generate an SSL certificate using OpenSSL:

```
$ openssl req -newkey rsa:2048 -nodes -keyout server-key.pem -out server-req.
    pem
$ openssl x509 -req -in server-req.pem -days 365 -signkey server-key.pem -out
    server-cert.pem
```

2. Copy the server-key.pem and server-cert.pem files to the MySQL server machine.

3. Edit the MySQL configuration file (my.cnf) and add the following

lines:

```
[mysqld]
ssl-ca=server-cert.pem
ssl-cert=server-cert.pem
ssl-key=server-key.pem
```

4. Restart the MySQL server.

To configure two-way SSL authentication in MySQL, you need to generate SSL certificates for both the client and the server and configure MySQL to use them. Here are the steps to follow:

1. Generate an SSL certificate for the server using OpenSSL as described above.

2. Generate an SSL certificate for the client using OpenSSL:

```
$ openssl req -newkey rsa:2048 -nodes -keyout client-key.pem -out client-req.
    pem
$ openssl x509 -req -in client-req.pem -days 365 -signkey client-key.pem -out
    client-cert.pem
```

3. Copy the client-key.pem and client-cert.pem files to the client machine.

4. Copy the server-key.pem and server-cert.pem files to the MySQL server machine.

5. Edit the MySQL configuration file (my.cnf) and add the following lines:

```
[mysqld]
ssl-ca=server-cert.pem
ssl-cert=server-cert.pem
ssl-key=server-key.pem
ssl-ca=client-cert.pem
ssl-cert=client-cert.pem
ssl-key=client-key.pem
```

6. Restart the MySQL server.

In conclusion, SSL authentication is an essential feature of MySQL that provides secure communication between the client and the server. One-way SSL authentication requires the client to authenticate the server, while two-way SSL authentication requires both the client and the server to authenticate each other. To configure SSL authentication in MySQL, you need to generate SSL certificates for the client and the server and configure MySQL to use them.

4.16   Can you explain the process of setting up and configuring master-slave replication in MySQL?

Setting up master-slave replication in MySQL involves the following steps:

1. **Setting up the master server**: To set up the master, you need to ensure that the 'log-bin' setting is enabled in the MySQL configuration file, which is usually located at '/etc/mysql/my.cnf' in Linux systems. To enable binary logging, add the following line to the '[mysqld]' section of the configuration file:

```
log-bin = mysql-bin
```

This tells MySQL to write all database changes to binary log files with a prefix of 'mysql-bin'. You'll also need to create a user account that the slave servers will use to connect to the master. For example, you can create a user named 'replication' and give it the necessary permissions:

```
CREATE USER 'replication'@'%' IDENTIFIED BY 'password';
GRANT REPLICATION SLAVE ON *.* TO 'replication'@'%';
```

2. **Setting up the slave server(s)**: Once the master server is configured, you'll need to set up the slave server(s). You can do this by editing the MySQL configuration file on each slave server, which is usually located at '/etc/mysql/my.cnf'. In addition to the usual MySQL settings, you'll need to add the following lines to the '[mysqld]' section:

```
server-id = <unique server ID>
relay-log = mysql-relay-bin
log-slave-updates = 1
```

The 'server-id' setting should be unique for each slave server, and can be any positive integer up to 232 - 1. The 'relay-log' setting tells MySQL to write relay logs that contain the changes received from the master. The 'log-slave-updates' setting tells MySQL to log any changes that are received from the master to its own binary log.

3. **Configuring the master for replication**: Once the server set-

tings are in place, you'll need to configure the master to allow replication. You can do this by logging in to the master server as the 'root' user and running the following commands:

```
FLUSH TABLES WITH READ LOCK;
SHOW MASTER STATUS;
```

The 'FLUSH TABLES WITH READ LOCK' command ensures that no database changes are made while you're setting up replication. The 'SHOW MASTER STATUS' command displays the 'File' and 'Position' values that you'll need later when configuring the slave.

4. **Configuring the slave for replication**: With the master configured, you can now set up replication on the slave server(s). Log in to each slave server as the 'root' user and run the following command:

```
CHANGE MASTER TO
  MASTER_HOST='<ip address or hostname of master>',
  MASTER_USER='replication',
  MASTER_PASSWORD='password',
  MASTER_LOG_FILE='<log file from SHOW MASTER STATUS>',
  MASTER_LOG_POS=<position from SHOW MASTER STATUS>;
```

This configures the slave to connect to the master server using the 'replication' user and the password you set up earlier. It also specifies the 'File' and 'Position' values obtained from 'SHOW MASTER STATUS'.

5. **Starting replication**: Once the master and slave are configured, you can start replication by running the following command on each slave server:

```
START SLAVE;
```

You can verify that replication is working by running 'SHOW SLAVE STATUS;' on the slave server. This should display a list of properties related to replication, including a 'Slave_IO_Running' and 'Slave_SQL_Running' field, which should both be set to 'Yes' if replication is working properly.

That's the general process for setting up master-slave replication in MySQL! Of course, there are many additional configuration options and best practices to consider depending on your specific use case and environment, but this should be a good starting point.

4.17   What is a database shard, and how does sharding help in scaling MySQL databases?

A database shard is a horizontal partition of data in a database, dividing the data into smaller and more manageable pieces called shards. Sharding is the process of breaking up a large database into smaller, independent units called shards, each with its own subset of data. This is done to improve performance, scalability, and availability of the database.

Sharding helps in scaling MySQL databases in a number of ways:

1. Improved performance: By dividing the data into smaller, more manageable pieces, queries can be executed across multiple shards in parallel, leading to faster query times.

2. Increased scalability: Sharding allows for the distribution of data across multiple servers, enabling MySQL databases to handle larger volumes of data and more concurrent connections.

3. Better availability: In a sharded environment, if a single shard goes down, only a portion of the data is affected, minimizing the impact on the entire system.

However, sharding also comes with some challenges, such as increased complexity in the configuration and management of the database, ensuring data consistency across shards, and dealing with hot spots where certain shards may receive a disproportionate amount of traffic.

To illustrate how sharding works in MySQL, consider the following example.

Suppose we have a table of customer orders with millions of rows, and we want to shard this table across multiple servers. We can use a sharding key, such as the customer ID, to determine which shard each order belongs to. For example, if we have two servers, we can shard the table as follows:

```
- Server 1: All orders with customer ID's from 1 to 500,000
- Server 2: All orders with customer ID's from 500,001 to 1,000,000
```

When a query is executed, the sharding middleware routes the query to the appropriate shard based on the customer ID in the WHERE clause. This allows the query to be executed on the specific shard that contains the relevant data, rather than scanning the entire table.

4.18 What are the benefits and challenges of using MySQL Cluster as a solution for high availability and scalability?

MySQL Cluster is a distributed, in-memory database designed to provide high-availability and scalability while maintaining data consistency. MySQL Cluster achieves this goal by dividing the data across multiple nodes and replicating it across all nodes in the cluster. In this way, it ensures that no single point of failure exists within the cluster, and the data is available even if some nodes fail.

Benefits:

- High Availability: MySQL Cluster is designed to provide 99.999% availability, which means that the database stays online even if some nodes go offline or become unavailable. MySQL Cluster ensures that if one node fails or goes down, another node can take over its responsibilities, and the database stays available to serve the requests
.
- Scalability: MySQL Cluster can scale horizontally by adding more nodes to the cluster. In this way, it can handle larger workloads and more concurrent users. As every node in the cluster can handle the transactions and queries, the addition of nodes increases the processing power of the cluster.
- High Performance: MySQL Cluster is an in-memory database that stores data in RAM. This makes it faster to read and write data as the data is available in the memory rather than on a physical disk. MySQL Cluster uses distributed query processing to ensure that the queries are processed on the nodes where the data resides. This reduces the network traffic and the load on the nodes.
- Data Consistency: MySQL Cluster uses synchronous replication to replicate data across all nodes in the cluster. This ensures that every node has consistent data and that the data is always available to all nodes.

Challenges:

- Complexity: MySQL Cluster is a complex database that requires specialized knowledge to set up and maintain. It requires a deep understanding of distributed systems, network configuration, and hardware optimization to ensure optimal performance and availability of the cluster.
- Cost: MySQL Cluster is a commercial product, and it requires a license to use. Depending on the size and requirements of the cluster, the licensing cost may be significant.
- Memory Requirement: As MySQL Cluster stores all data in memory, the memory requirement of the cluster is significant. The memory requirement increases with the size of the data and the number of nodes in the

```
     cluster.
   - Limited Functionality: MySQL Cluster is optimized for high-availability and
     scalability, but it may not be suitable for all types of applications.
     Some features, such as full-text search, may not be available in the
     cluster.
```

In conclusion, MySQL Cluster is a robust solution for high-availability and scalability, but it requires specialized knowledge to set up and maintain. It offers high performance, data consistency, and the ability to scale horizontally, but it also has significant memory requirements, licensing costs, and limited functionality. Therefore, it is essential to evaluate the requirements of the application before choosing MySQL Cluster as a solution for high availability and scalability.

4.19   How do you handle character set and collation issues in MySQL, especially when dealing with multilingual data?

In MySQL, character set and collation determine how the server stores, compares, and sorts character string data. Handling character set and collation issues is critical when dealing with multilingual data since different languages have different character sets and collations.

Here are some steps to handle character set and collation issues in MySQL when dealing with multilingual data:

1. Choose the Right Character Set:

MySQL supports a wide range of character sets, including Unicode, Latin, Cyrillic, and Asian character sets. When working with multilingual data, it is recommended to choose Unicode character set (UTF-8) that can store characters from all major languages in the world.

To specify the character set for a database, use the following SQL command:

```
CREATE DATABASE mydb CHARACTER SET utf8;
```

This command creates a database named 'mydb' with the UTF-8 character set.

2. Choose the Right Collation:

Collation determines how the server compares and sorts character string data. It defines the order in which characters appear in a sorted list. MySQL supports a wide range of collations for each character set. When working with multilingual data, it is recommended to choose a collation that supports the specific language you are dealing with.

For example, if you are dealing with German language, you can choose the 'utf8_german2_ci' collation that supports German language-specific sorting rules.

To specify the collation for a table, use the following SQL command:

```
CREATE TABLE mytable (
  id INT PRIMARY KEY AUTO_INCREMENT,
  name VARCHAR(50) CHARACTER SET utf8 COLLATE utf8_german2_ci
);
```

3. Convert Existing Data:

If you have existing data that uses a different character set or collation, you can convert it to the desired character set and collation using the 'ALTER TABLE' command. For example, to convert a table named 'mytable' to use the UTF-8 character set and the 'utf8_general_ci' collation, use the following SQL command:

```
ALTER TABLE mytable CONVERT TO CHARACTER SET utf8 COLLATE utf8_general_ci;
```

4. Use Prepared Statements:

When inserting or updating multilingual data, it is recommended to use prepared statements to make sure that the data is properly encoded and escaped. Prepared statements automatically handle character set encoding and escaping, which can prevent SQL injection attacks.

Here is an example of using prepared statements with multilingual data:

```
$mysqli = new mysqli("localhost", "username", "password", "mydb");

$stmt = $mysqli->prepare("INSERT INTO mytable (name) VALUES (?)");
```

```
$stmt->bind_param("s", $name);

$name = "Japanese␣Text...";
$stmt->execute();

$name = "Russina␣Text...";
$stmt->execute();

$stmt->close();
$mysqli->close();
```

In this example, prepared statements are used to insert two Japanese and Russian strings into a table named 'mytable'.

In conclusion, handling character set and collation issues is critical when dealing with multilingual data in MySQL. It is important to choose the right character set and collation, convert existing data, and use prepared statements to ensure that the data is properly encoded and safe.

4.20   How do you use MySQL's window functions like ROW_NUMBER(), RANK(), and DENSE_RANK() for advanced data analysis?

MySQL's window functions are powerful tools for advanced data analysis. These functions allow you to perform calculations on a subset of the data, rather than the entire dataset. In this way, you can easily calculate rankings, running totals, and other calculations that require working with subsets of data.

In MySQL, Row_number(), rank() and dense_rank() are three window functions that are particularly useful for data analysis. These functions allow you to add a ranking to a select statement based on a specific column.

Usage of ROW_NUMBER()

The row_number() function assigns a unique number to each row within a result set, starting with 1 for the first row. This function is useful for pagination, subsetting data within a result set, or tracking the order in which data is returned.

Here is an example of using row_number() to return the top 10 highest-paid employees from a salary table:

```
SELECT first_name, last_name, salary,
ROW_NUMBER() OVER (ORDER BY salary DESC) AS rank
FROM employee
WHERE salary IS NOT NULL
ORDER BY rank ASC LIMIT 10
```

This query will return the first 10 rows of the result set, with each row assigned a rank value based on the salary.

Usage of RANK()

The RANK() function assigns a rank to each row within a result set, based on the values of a column. If two rows have the same value, they will receive the same rank, with the next rank being skipped.

Here is an example of using rank() to return the top 5 salespeople based on their sales:

```
SELECT first_name, last_name, sales,
RANK() OVER (ORDER BY sales DESC) AS rank
FROM salespeople
WHERE sales IS NOT NULL
ORDER BY rank ASC LIMIT 5
```

This query will return the first 5 rows of the result set, with each row assigned a rank value based on the sales.

Usage of DENSE_RANK()

The DENSE_RANK() function is similar to rank(), but it assigns a rank to each row within a result set, based on the values of a column. If two rows have the same value, they will receive the same rank, and no rank will be skipped.

Here is an example of using dense_rank() to return the top 10 cities with the most users:

```
SELECT city, COUNT(*) AS num_users,
```

```
DENSE_RANK() OVER (ORDER BY COUNT(*) DESC) AS rank
FROM users
GROUP BY city
ORDER BY rank ASC LIMIT 10
```

This query will return the top 10 cities based on the number of users, with each row assigned a rank value based on the number of users. If two cities have the same number of users, they will receive the same rank, and no rank will be skipped.

In conclusion, MySQL's window functions are powerful tools for advanced data analysis. They allow you to perform calculations on a subset of the data, rather than the entire dataset. The ROW_NUMBER(), RANK(), and DENSE_RANK() functions are particularly useful for calculating rankings and running totals. These functions are easy to use and can help to simplify complex SQL queries.

Chapter 5

Expert

5.1 What are the key differences between MySQL and other database systems like PostgreSQL and SQL Server in terms of performance and features?

MySQL, PostgreSQL, and SQL Server are all popular database systems used in various applications. Here are some key differences between these database systems in terms of performance and features:

Performance:

- MySQL is known for its fast performance and scalability. It is designed to handle a large number of concurrent connections and is optimized for read-heavy workloads.

- PostgreSQL also offers high performance and scalability but is optimized for write-heavy workloads. It has advanced indexing capabilities that allow it to handle complex queries efficiently.

- SQL Server is known for its enterprise-level performance and scalability. It is designed to handle large and complex databases with high-speed transactions.

Features:

- MySQL supports most standard SQL features, but lacks some advanced features such as recursive queries and window functions. It has a strong focus on simple data storage and retrieval, making it an ideal choice for web applications.

- PostgreSQL offers a wide range of advanced features, including advanced indexing, JSON support, and support for key-value stores. It also supports recursive queries and window functions, making it a popular choice for data analytics.

- SQL Server offers enterprise-level features such as high availability, disaster recovery, and advanced security features. It also offers support for advanced data analytics features such as machine learning and data mining.

Here are some examples of performance and feature differences in action:

- If you are building a web application with a heavy read workload, MySQL may be the best option due to its fast performance.

- If you are building a data analytics platform that requires advanced features such as recursive queries and window functions, PostgreSQL may be the best option.

- If you are building an enterprise-level application that requires high availability and disaster recovery features, SQL Server may be the best option.

Overall, the choice of database system depends on the specific needs and requirements of the application being built.

5.2   How do you perform query optimization using MySQL's query rewrite plugins?

MySQL's query optimizer is a powerful tool that can help database administrators and developers to optimize queries for better performance. One way to optimize queries is through the use of query rewrite plugins. A query rewrite plugin is a custom plugin that modifies queries before they are executed by the MySQL server. In this way, developers can modify queries to use alternative execution paths or to remove unnecessary calculations, making them faster and more efficient.

Here are the steps to perform query optimization using MySQL's query rewrite plugins:

1. Identify the queries that need optimization: Before you can optimize a query, you need to identify which queries are causing performance issues. You can use tools like MySQL's slow query log, performance schema, or third-party monitoring tools to identify queries that are taking longer to execute.

2. Choose a query rewrite plugin: MySQL comes with several built-in query rewrite plugins, including the simple_query_rewrite, audit_rewrite, and oqgraph. You can also create your own custom query rewrite plugins based on your application's specific needs.

3. Write the query rewrite plugin: Once you have chosen a query rewrite plugin, you need to write the code that will modify the queries. This involves using the appropriate MySQL API to parse the query, identify the parts that need to be modified, and then rewrite the query.

Here is an example of a simple query rewrite plugin:

```
CREATE FUNCTION my_query_rewrite_plugin(query TEXT) RETURNS TEXT
BEGIN
  -- Check if the query needs to be modified
  IF INSTR(query, 'SELECT * FROM products WHERE price > 100') > 0 THEN
    SET query = REPLACE(query, 'SELECT * FROM products WHERE price > 100', '
      SELECT * FROM products WHERE price > 50');
  END IF;

  -- Return the modified query
  RETURN query;
END;
```

In this example, the plugin modifies any queries that retrieve data from the "products" table where the price is greater than 100. It replaces the "price > 100" condition with "price > 50" to reduce the number of rows retrieved from the database.

4. Install and configure the query rewrite plugin: Once you have written your query rewrite plugin, you need to install and configure it in MySQL. This involves creating a shared library that contains your plugin code, adding the library to the MySQL plugin directory, and then configuring the plugin in MySQL's configuration file.

5. Test and measure the performance: Once the plugin is installed and configured, you can test it by running the queries that you identified in step 1. Measure the performance of the queries before and after the plugin is applied to see the improvement in query execution time.

In conclusion, MySQL's query rewrite plugins are a powerful tool that can help optimize queries and improve performance. By identifying slow queries, choosing the appropriate plugin, writing the plugin code, installing and configuring the plugin, and testing the performance, developers can significantly improve the efficiency of their MySQL database.

5.3   How do you plan and execute a smooth MySQL version upgrade with minimal downtime and risks?

Upgrading MySQL version can be a daunting task if not planned and executed properly, but with proper planning, it can be done with minimal downtime and risks. The following are some steps to plan and execute a smooth MySQL version upgrade:

Step 1: Understanding the current MySQL implementation
Before upgrading MySQL, it is important to understand the current implementation. This involves gathering information about the current MySQL version, checking the compatibility of the new MySQL version, understanding the database schema and design, and noting down the customizations and configurations made in the current implementation. By doing this, possible issues and risks can be identified and mitigated in advance.

Step 2: Testing the upgrade process
Before upgrading the production environment, it is important to test the upgrade process in a staging or test environment. This can help in understanding the potential issues that may be faced during the actual upgrade process. In the test environment, one can upgrade MySQL version, test the database schema, and applications compatibility with the new version.

Step 3: Preparing for the upgrade

After testing the upgrade process and understanding the current MySQL implementation, the next step is to prepare for the upgrade. This involves taking backup of the current MySQL, understanding the rollback plan, and getting the resources needed for the actual upgrade process.

Step 4: Executing the upgrade process
The actual upgrade process should be carried out with minimal downtime and risks. This can be achieved by following the steps:

- Stop MySQL server and services

- Backup the current MySQL version

- Install the new MySQL version and configure it based on the previous configuration.

- Upgrade the data files with the mysql_upgrade utility

- Verify the new MySQL version installation and database schema

- Start MySQL server and services

Step 5: Testing and verification After the upgrade process, it is important to test the database schema, functionality, applications compatibility, and performance. This is done to ensure that everything works as expected and there are no inconsistencies or issues.

In conclusion, upgrading MySQL version requires proper planning and execution to minimize downtime and risks. By understanding the current MySQL implementation, testing the upgrade process, preparing for the upgrade, executing the upgrade process, and testing and verification, one can upgrade MySQL version smoothly.

5.4 How do you use the Global Transaction Identifier (GTID) in MySQL replication, and what are its benefits?

Global Transaction Identifier (GTID) is a unique identifier assigned to each transaction executed on the master in MySQL. GTID is important because it simplifies replication and makes it easier to manage failover.

First, let's discuss the format of the GTID. It consists of three parts:

```
source_id:transaction_id
```

- 'source_id' is a unique identifier for each server in a replication topology.

- 'transaction_id' is an incremental number assigned to each transaction on the source server.

Now let's discuss how GTID is used in MySQL replication. In a replication topology, each slave tracks the GTID of the last transaction processed. Whenever a slave connects to a master, it sends its GTID position to the master, and the master starts sending transactions starting from that point. This eliminates the need for a slave to keep track of the binary log file and position.

GTID has several benefits over traditional binary log and position-based replication:

1. Simplified failover: In case of failover, the new master can easily continue replication from the last known GTID position, without having to worry about which binary log file and position to start from.

2. Easier to manage multi-source replication: With GTID, it's easy to track transactions from multiple sources and avoid conflicts.

3. Better detection of conflicts: With traditional replication, conflicts can occur if a transaction is executed on multiple servers with different binary log coordinates. GTID eliminates this problem by providing a unique identifier for each transaction.

To use GTID in MySQL replication, you need to enable it on both the master and the slave servers. To enable GTID on the master, add the following lines to your my.cnf file:

```
server-id=1
log-bin
enforce-gtid-consistency
```

The 'enforce-gtid-consistency' option ensures that all transactions are assigned a GTID.

To enable GTID on the slave, add the following line to your my.cnf file:

```
server-id=2
enforce-gtid-consistency
```

Then, start replication as usual, using the 'CHANGE MASTER TO' command. You'll need to specify the master server's GTID position:

```
CHANGE MASTER TO MASTER_HOST='master', MASTER_PORT=3306, MASTER_USER='
    replication', MASTER_PASSWORD='secret', MASTER_AUTO_POSITION=1;
```

The 'MASTER_AUTO_POSITION' option tells the slave to use the master's GTID position.

In conclusion, GTID simplifies replication and makes it easier to manage failover and multi-source replication. It's a powerful tool that is becoming increasingly popular in MySQL replication.

5.5   What is the role of the InnoDB buffer pool size in MySQL performance tuning, and how do you configure it appropriately?

The InnoDB buffer pool is a key component in the MySQL database engine. It is a cache that stores data and indexes in memory, making database operations faster by reducing the I/O operations required to access data from the disk. The InnoDB buffer pool size determines the amount of memory allocated for this purpose.

Configuring the InnoDB buffer pool size appropriately is crucial for ensuring optimal performance in a MySQL database. The general rule of thumb is to allocate as much memory as possible to the buffer pool without causing the system to swap memory to disk.

The following formula is commonly used to estimate the appropriate size of the InnoDB buffer pool:

$$innodb\_buffer\_pool\_size = \frac{Total\_Memory - OS\_Memory - Other\_Programs\_Memory}{2}$$

Where:

- Total_Memory: the amount of memory available on the system

- OS_Memory: the amount of memory required by the operating system

- Other_Programs_Memory: the amount of memory required by other running programs

For example, if a system has 16GB of RAM and the OS and other programs require 4GB of memory, then the recommended InnoDB buffer pool size would be 6GB ((16GB - 4GB) / 2).

In addition to the above formula, there are some other factors to consider when configuring the InnoDB buffer pool size:

- Workload: The amount of data and the type of queries being executed can have a significant impact on the buffer pool size. A database that primarily runs read queries may require a larger buffer pool than one that runs mostly write queries.

- Connection pooling: The number of connections to the database can also impact the buffer pool size. If a large number of connections are being made concurrently, a larger buffer pool may be required.

To configure the InnoDB buffer pool size, the following steps can be taken:

1. Check the current buffer pool size by running the following command in the MySQL workbench:

```
SHOW VARIABLES LIKE 'innodb_buffer_pool_size';
```

2. Determine the appropriate buffer pool size based on the system's RAM, OS and other program requirements, and workload.

3. Update the MySQL configuration file (my.cnf or my.ini) with the appropriate buffer pool size.

```
[mysqld]
innodb_buffer_pool_size = 6G
```

4. Restart the MySQL server to apply the changes.

In conclusion, the InnoDB buffer pool size plays a critical role in MySQL performance tuning as it can significantly impact the speed and efficiency of database operations. Configuring the buffer pool size appropriately involves a number of factors, including available memory, workload, and number of connections, and should be closely monitored and adjusted as necessary to ensure optimal performance.

5.6 Can you explain the concept of Multi-Version Concurrency Control (MVCC) in MySQL, and how does it affect transaction isolation levels?

Multi-Version Concurrency Control (MVCC) is a technique used to allow multiple concurrent transactions to read and write data in a database without interfering with each other. This approach is used in many databases, including MySQL.

In MVCC, each transaction sees a snapshot of the database at the time of the query's start, rather than the current state of the database. This means that each transaction sees a consistent view of the database, even when other transactions are modifying the same data.

MVCC works by keeping multiple versions of each row in the database. Each version of a row is marked with a timestamp, and when a transaction reads a row, it sees the version with the highest timestamp that is older than the transaction's start time. If a transaction modifies a row, it creates a new version of the row with a new timestamp.

The different transaction isolation levels in MySQL determine the degree to which one transaction can see changes made by other transactions. The four standard transaction isolation levels in MySQL are:

1. READ UNCOMMITTED: This level allows transactions to read data that has been modified by other transactions but not yet committed. This level can result in dirty reads, which means that a transaction can read data that ends up being rolled back by another transaction, causing the first transaction to read invalid data.

2. READ COMMITTED: This level allows transactions to read only data that has been committed by other transactions. This level avoids dirty reads but can produce non-repeatable reads, which means that the same query may return different results at different times because

the data may have been modified by other transactions.

3. REPEATABLE READ: This level ensures that a transaction sees
the same data throughout its execution. This means that the transaction will not see changes made by other transactions that occur
after the transaction starts. This level avoids both dirty reads and
non-repeatable reads.

4. SERIALIZABLE: This level provides the highest degree of isolation
and ensures that transactions are executed in a serializable order.
This means that even though multiple transactions may attempt to
modify the same data simultaneously, the results will be the same as if
they were executed in a serial order. This level avoids all consistency
problems but can be slower because transactions must wait for each
other to complete.

In summary, MVCC allows concurrent transactions to operate on the
same data without interfering with each other by keeping multiple
versions of each row in the database. The different transaction isolation levels in MySQL determine the degree to which one transaction
can see changes made by other transactions. Each level has different
trade-offs in terms of consistency and performance.

5.7   What is MySQL Group Replication, and how does it differ from traditional master-slave replication in terms of consistency and fault tolerance?

MySQL Group Replication is a plugin that enables synchronous replication in a group of MySQL servers, providing fault-tolerant, highly
available distributed storage with automatic synchronization. It is
based on a new replication protocol with a group membership service, which ensures that all servers have an up-to-date copy of the
data. This technology was introduced in MySQL 5.7.17 and is a
built-in component in the MySQL Community edition.

Group Replication has several advantages over traditional master-
slave replication in terms of consistency and fault tolerance. First,

it provides a more consistent view of the database across all nodes. In traditional master-slave replication, there is typically one master server that handles all writes and updates to the database, and multiple slave servers that receive copies of the data. This can result in delays or inconsistencies in replication, leading to potentially different data sets on different nodes.

In Group Replication, all nodes are equal peers and have the same level of authority to accept updates. This makes it possible for clients to write or read to any node in the group, and any updates will be propagated to all other nodes in real-time, making sure the data is always consistent across all nodes.

Second, Group Replication provides fault tolerance by allowing the group to continue functioning even if some nodes fail or are temporarily unavailable. In traditional master-slave replication, if the master fails, the entire system becomes unavailable until the master is replaced. In Group Replication, if a node fails, a new node can be added to the group to replace it, and data will continue to be available without interruption.

Group Replication uses a Multi-Master topology, where all nodes in the group act as masters and receive updates from other nodes in real-time. This means that any node can accept updates, and those updates are automatically propagated to other nodes in the group. The fault-tolerant nature of the group is achieved through group membership management, where each node is aware of the status of other nodes in the group.

In conclusion, MySQL Group Replication provides a more consistent and fault-tolerant replication method compared to traditional master-slave replication. It ensures that all nodes have an up-to-date copy of the data and can accept updates independently, making it much more resilient to failures of single nodes.

5.8   How do you configure and use MySQL's semi-synchronous replication to achieve a balance between data durability and performance?

MySQL's semi-synchronous replication feature ensures that a transaction is committed to the upstream master and at least one replica before the user is notified that a write operation has succeeded, providing a balance between data durability and performance.

To configure MySQL's semi-synchronous replication, the following steps need to be taken:

1. Enable semi-synchronous replication on the master server by setting the "rpl_semi_sync_master_enabled" variable to true:

```
mysql> SET GLOBAL rpl_semi_sync_master_enabled = 1;
```

2. Enable semi-synchronous replication on the replica server(s) by setting the "rpl_semi_sync_slave_enabled" variable to true:

```
mysql> SET GLOBAL rpl_semi_sync_slave_enabled = 1;
```

3. Set the "rpl_semi_sync_master_wait_for_slave_count" variable to the number of replicas you want to wait for before considering the write operation successful. For instance, to wait for one replica, set the value to 1:

```
mysql> SET GLOBAL rpl_semi_sync_master_wait_for_slave_count = 1;
```

4. Start the MySQL server on the replica server(s).

After configuring the semi-synchronous replication feature, write operations will now behave differently. When a client issues a write operation, the following will happen:

1. The master server receives the write operation and immediately sends an acknowledgement to the client that the write operation succeeded.

2. The master server waits for at least one replica to acknowledge

receipt of the write operation by sending a "commit" message back to the master.

3. Once the master server receives an acknowledgement from at least one replica, the transaction is considered complete.

By waiting for a replica to acknowledge receipt of the write operation before considering it successful, we achieve a balance between data durability and performance. However, this comes at the cost of increased latency, as the client has to wait for the master to receive an acknowledgement from at least one replica.

It's important to note that semi-synchronous replication doesn't guarantee that the data is fully replicated to all replicas at the time of acknowledgement. There is still some data loss risk if the master server crashes before the write operation is fully propagated to all replicas.

In conclusion, MySQL's semi-synchronous replication is a useful feature for achieving a balance between data durability and performance. By configuring it correctly, you can increase the durability of your data without sacrificing too much performance.

5.9 What are some common issues related to MySQL replication lag, and how do you mitigate them?

MySQL replication is used to replicate data from one MySQL instance, also known as the master, to one or more instances, also known as the slaves. It is an important feature of MySQL that helps to maintain data consistency and availability. However, there are common issues related to MySQL replication lag that may occur during the replication process, and they can be caused by a number of factors like network latency, hardware issues, configuration issues, etc. In this answer, we will discuss some of these issues and how to mitigate them.

1. Network latency: Network latency is the amount of time it takes for data to travel from the master to the slave. This can be a major cause

of replication lag if the network is slow or congested. To mitigate this issue, you can consider the following:

- Ensure that the network connection between the master and slaves is fast and reliable.

- Use replication settings to reduce network traffic and improve replication speed, such as setting the "slave_compressed_protocol" option to compress the data being transmitted between the master and slave.

2. Hardware issues: Hardware issues can also cause replication lag, particularly if the slave server is underpowered, has insufficient memory or disk space, or is experiencing high I/O usage. To mitigate this issue, you can consider the following:

- Ensure that the slave hardware is capable of handling the amount of data being replicated from the master.

- Tune the MySQL settings on the slave server to optimize performance and reduce I/O usage, such as increasing the "innodb_buffer_pool_size" setting.

3. Configuration issues: Configuration issues can also cause replication lag, particularly if the MySQL settings on the master and slave servers are not optimized for replication. To mitigate this issue, you can consider the following:

- Review and optimize the MySQL configuration settings on both the master and slave servers.

- Ensure that the server clocks are synchronized, as a difference in clock time between the master and slave can cause replication to lag.

4. Long-running queries: Long-running queries on the master can cause replication lag on the slave servers, as they can hold up the replication process. To mitigate this issue, you can consider the following:

- Ensure that the master server is optimized for performance, particularly the queries that are most likely to cause replication lag.

- Use tools like "pt-kill" to terminate long-running queries on the master.

In conclusion, MySQL replication lag can be caused by a number of factors, including network latency, hardware issues, configuration issues, and long-running queries. To mitigate these issues, it is important to ensure that the network and hardware are optimized for replication, that the MySQL settings are configured correctly, and that long-running queries are addressed.

5.10 How do you design and implement an efficient and scalable MySQL architecture using sharding, replication, and caching techniques?

Designing an efficient and scalable MySQL architecture requires careful consideration of several factors such as data size, traffic patterns, availability requirements, latency requirements, and budget. In this answer, I will discuss how sharding, replication, and caching techniques can be used to achieve scalability and performance in a MySQL architecture.

Sharding

Sharding is a technique used to distribute data across multiple servers. It involves partitioning the data into smaller subsets and assigning each subset to a different server. Sharding helps to distribute the load evenly across multiple servers and enables the system to handle more traffic and data size.

Horizontal vs. Vertical Sharding

There are two types of sharding: horizontal and vertical sharding. Horizontal sharding involves splitting the data horizontally across multiple servers based on a certain criteria such as user ID, region, or date range. Vertical sharding involves splitting the data vertically into smaller subsets based on specific columns such as the most frequently accessed columns.

Choosing a Sharding Key

Choosing the right sharding key is critical for efficient sharding. The sharding key determines how the data is partitioned across different servers. The ideal sharding key should have a high cardinality and evenly distributed data. For example, if we are sharding a user table based on user ID, we want to make sure that the user IDs are evenly distributed across different servers and there are no hotspots.

Implementing Sharding

Implementing sharding in MySQL requires the use of a sharding middleware such as MySQL Proxy or Vitess. The sharding middleware sits between the application and the MySQL servers and routes the queries to the appropriate server based on the sharding key.

Replication

Replication is a technique used to create multiple copies of the data across different servers. It is used to achieve high availability, disaster recovery, and read scalability.

Master-Slave Replication

The most common form of replication is master-slave replication. In this architecture, one server acts as the master and accepts write operations, while multiple servers act as slaves and replicate the data from the master. The slaves can be used for read operations to achieve read scalability.

Master-Master Replication

Master-master replication is another form of replication where multiple servers act as masters and accept write operations. This architecture is used for high availability and load balancing. However, it requires careful configuration to avoid conflicts when multiple masters try to write to the same data.

Implementing Replication

Implementing replication in MySQL involves configuring the master and slave servers and setting up replication channels. The replication channels are used to transfer the data from the master to the slave servers. MySQL provides built-in support for replication, and there are also third-party tools such as Percona XtraBackup that can simplify the replication setup.

Caching

Caching is a technique used to store frequently accessed data in memory to reduce the latency of read operations. Caching can be implemented in different layers of the architecture, such as the application layer, the database layer, or the network layer.

Application Layer Caching

Application layer caching involves storing frequently accessed data in memory within the application. This requires modifying the application code to implement the caching logic. Popular caching solutions for the application layer include Memcached and Redis.

Database Layer Caching

Database layer caching involves storing frequently accessed data in memory within the database server. This can be achieved using MySQL's built-in query cache or third-party solutions such as ProxySQL or Nginx with the ngx_cache_purge module.

Network Layer Caching

Network layer caching involves caching frequently accessed data in memory within a caching server such as Varnish or CDN. This can be used to reduce the load on the application and database servers by serving cached content directly from the network layer.

Conclusion

Designing an efficient and scalable MySQL architecture requires a combination of sharding, replication, and caching techniques. Sharding helps distribute data across multiple servers, replication provides high availability and read scalability, and caching reduces the latency of read operations. Choosing the right sharding and caching key is critical for efficient sharding and caching. Implementing these techniques requires careful configuration and choosing the right tools and middleware.

5.11   How do you use the ProxySQL load balancer to optimize performance and manage connections in a MySQL environment?

ProxySQL is a powerful open-source proxy for MySQL that can be used to manage and optimize connections in a MySQL environment. ProxySQL acts as an intermediary between the MySQL server and clients, allowing for efficient connection management and load balancing.

To use ProxySQL in a MySQL environment, follow these steps:

1. Install and configure ProxySQL: The first step is to install and configure ProxySQL. ProxySQL can be installed on any server that has access to the MySQL servers that it will manage. ProxySQL uses a configuration file to determine its behavior, which can be customized to suit the needs of your environment.

2. Configure ProxySQL to manage MySQL connections: Once ProxySQL is installed and configured, the next step is to configure it to manage MySQL connections. This involves creating MySQL users and defining the rules for how MySQL connections should be handled. For example, you can configure ProxySQL to send read-only queries to a particular server, while write queries are sent to a different server.

3. Configure ProxySQL for load balancing: ProxySQL can be used to balance the load across multiple MySQL servers. This involves defining rules for how queries should be distributed across the MySQL servers. For example, you might set up a rule that sends read-only queries to the least busy server, while write queries are sent to the server with the most available connections.

4. Monitor and manage ProxySQL: Finally, it's important to monitor and manage ProxySQL to ensure that it's performing as expected. This involves monitoring ProxySQL's logs and metrics to identify potential issues, and tweaking the configuration as necessary to optimize performance.

Here's an example of how to use ProxySQL to balance the load across multiple MySQL servers. First, we'll create three MySQL servers:

```
CREATE DATABASE db;
GRANT ALL PRIVILEGES ON db.* TO 'user'@'localhost' IDENTIFIED BY 'password';
```

Next, we'll configure ProxySQL to manage these servers:

```
INSERT INTO mysql_servers (hostgroup_id, hostname, port) VALUES (1, 'mysql1',
    3306);
INSERT INTO mysql_servers (hostgroup_id, hostname, port) VALUES (1, 'mysql2',
    3306);
INSERT INTO mysql_servers (hostgroup_id, hostname, port) VALUES (1, 'mysql3',
    3306);

INSERT INTO mysql_users (username, password, default_hostgroup) VALUES ('user
    ', 'password', 1);

INSERT INTO mysql_query_rules (rule_id, match_pattern, destination_hostgroup)
    VALUES (1, '^SELECT', 1);
INSERT INTO mysql_query_rules (rule_id, match_pattern, destination_hostgroup)
    VALUES (2, '.*', 2);
```

In this example, we've configured ProxySQL to send SELECT queries to the first MySQL server, and all other queries to the second MySQL server.

By using ProxySQL to manage MySQL connections, you can dramatically improve the performance and scalability of your MySQL environment.

5.12   How do you monitor and analyze slow query logs in MySQL to identify performance bottlenecks and optimize queries?

Monitoring and analyzing slow query logs in MySQL is crucial for identifying performance bottlenecks and optimizing queries. Slow query logs record all queries that take longer than a specified time threshold to execute. In MySQL, slow queries are logged in a file usually named "slow-query.log". This file can be analyzed to track down and optimize queries that are causing performance issues.

Here are the steps to monitor and analyze slow query logs in MySQL:

1. Enable slow query log

The first step in monitoring slow query logs is to enable them. You can enable slow query logs by adding the following lines in your MySQL configuration file 'my.cnf':

```
slow_query_log = 1
slow_query_log_file = /var/log/mysql/slow-query.log
long_query_time = 1 #The time in seconds it takes to execute a query before
    it is logged
```

Once you have added these lines, you need to restart the MySQL server for the changes to take effect.

2. Analyze the slow query log

After enabling the slow query log, MySQL will start logging all queries that take longer than the specified time to execute. You can access the slow query log by navigating to the location specified in the 'slow_query_log_file' parameter.

The slow query log will contain all queries that took longer than the specified time to execute, along with additional information like the query execution time, number of rows examined and sent, and the query execution plan. You can use this information to identify queries that are causing performance issues.

Here is an example of a slow query log entry:

```
# Time: 2021-05-06T17:58:34.198083Z
# User@Host: root[root] @ localhost [] Id: 2
# Query_time: 2.112185 Lock_time: 0.000000 Rows_sent: 10 Rows_examined:
    1000361
SET timestamp=1620292714;
SELECT * FROM orders WHERE order_date BETWEEN '2021-01-01' AND '2021-04-30';
```

In this example, we can see that the query took 2.112 seconds to execute and examined over 1 million rows. This query could be a potential bottleneck that needs to be optimized.

3. Optimize slow queries

Once you have identified slow queries that are causing performance issues, you can optimize them to improve performance. The first step in optimizing queries is to analyze the query execution plan. The execution plan shows the steps that MySQL takes to execute the query and helps identify where the query is spending the most time.

You can use the 'EXPLAIN' statement in MySQL to view the query execution plan. For example:

```
EXPLAIN SELECT * FROM orders WHERE order_date BETWEEN '2021-01-01' AND '
    2021-04-30';
```

The 'EXPLAIN' statement will show the tables used in the query, the order in which they are joined, and the indexes used. You can use this information to identify potential areas for optimization, such as missing indexes or inefficient join operations.

Once you have identified areas for optimization, you can modify the query to improve performance. For example, you can add indexes to columns that are frequently used in the query or rewrite the query to use more efficient join operations.

In conclusion, monitoring and analyzing slow query logs in MySQL is critical for identifying performance bottlenecks and optimizing queries. By following the above steps, you can identify slow queries and optimize them to improve performance.

5.13 What are some advanced strategies for schema design in MySQL to improve performance and maintainability?

There are several advanced strategies for schema design in MySQL that can improve performance and maintainability. These include:

1) Normalization:
Normalization refers to the process of splitting up a database into smaller, more manageable tables to reduce redundancy and maintain data integrity. Normalization can help improve performance because it reduces data duplication and ensures that data is stored in the most appropriate table. For example, a customer's name, address, and phone number may be stored in a separate table from their orders to avoid unnecessary duplication of data.

2) Denormalization:
Denormalization refers to the process of intentionally introducing re-

dundancy into a database to improve performance. This technique is often used in read-heavy applications where the cost of processing queries outweighs the cost of storing redundant data. For example, if an application needs to display a customer's complete order history on a single page, it may be useful to denormalize the data and store it in a single table.

3) Partitioning:
Partitioning refers to the process of splitting up a large table into smaller, more manageable pieces. This can improve performance by reducing the amount of data that needs to be scanned for a single query. For example, a table that contains millions of rows may be partitioned into smaller chunks based on date ranges or other criteria.

4) Indexing:
Indexing is the process of creating indexes on one or more columns in a table to speed up data retrieval. Indexes can help improve performance by allowing the database to quickly locate data without having to scan the entire table. However, adding too many indexes can also slow down write operations and increase the size of the database.

5) Compression:
Compression refers to the process of reducing the amount of space needed to store data in a database. This can improve performance by reducing the amount of disk I/O needed to read and write data. However, compression can also increase the CPU usage needed to decompress data, so it's important to balance the benefits of compression with its potential drawbacks.

6) Caching:
Caching refers to the process of temporarily storing frequently accessed data in memory to reduce the amount of disk I/O needed to read and write data. This can improve performance by reducing the time needed to retrieve data from disk. However, caching can also increase the memory usage of the database server and may require more frequent updates to ensure data consistency.

Overall, the key to designing a high-performance and maintainable database schema in MySQL is to carefully consider the tradeoffs between different design choices and choose the approach that best fits the needs of the application. It's also important to monitor the performance of the database over time and make adjustments as needed to ensure that it continues to meet the needs of the users.

5.14 How do you manage database migrations in large-scale MySQL environments to minimize risks and ensure consistency?

Database migrations are a common task in a database environment. As the database evolves over time, changes must be made to the database schema, data types, and indexes, among others. Large-scale MySQL environments are especially prone to database migrations, both in terms of frequency and complexity.

To minimize risks and ensure consistency when managing database migrations in large-scale MySQL environments, the following best practices can be applied:

1. Use a version control system
Using a version control system to manage database schema changes can help to track all changes, review and compare changes, and roll back changes as needed. Git is a popular version control system widely used in software development, and it can be used to manage database schema changes as well. Changes to the database schema can be done in a separate branch, and then merged into the main branch once testing is completed.

2. Create a migration plan
A migration plan outlines the steps required to make database schema changes. It should include steps for both the pre-migration and post-migration phases, such as testing, backup, and monitoring. The migration plan should also include a rollback plan in case of any errors or issues during the migration.

3. Test the migration
Testing the migration is critical to ensure that the database schema changes are successful and don't cause any issues. Testing should be done on a copy of the production database using a test environment. Quality assurance (QA) testing can also be conducted to ensure that

the applications that use the database continue to function as expected.

4. Back up the database
Back up the production database before performing the migration. This can help to restore the database to its original state in case of any issues during the migration. Backup can be done using standard tools such as mysqldump or through database replication.

5. Monitor the migration
During the migration, monitor the database and related systems to ensure that everything is functioning as expected. This includes monitoring performance, server resources, and log files for any errors.

6. Document the migration
Document the database schema changes and migration steps for future reference. This can help to maintain consistency and ensure that database administrators understand the changes made to the database schema.

In conclusion, managing database migrations in large-scale MySQL environments can be complex, but following best practices such as using a version control system, creating a migration plan, testing the migration, backing up the database, monitoring the migration, and documenting the migration can minimize risks and ensure consistency.

5.15 How do you use the mysqlpump utility for efficient and parallelized MySQL backups?

The 'mysqlpump' utility is a powerful backup tool that is included in MySQL 5.7 and later versions. It allows you to take efficient and parallelized backups of your MySQL databases. In this answer, we will explain how to use the 'mysqlpump' utility for efficient and parallelized MySQL backups.

Before we start, it's important to note that the 'mysqlpump' utility uses the InnoDB storage engine, so if you have any MyISAM tables, you'll need to convert them to InnoDB before using 'mysqlpump'.

To use 'mysqlpump', follow these steps:

1. Open a terminal or command prompt and navigate to the location where you want to store your backup files.

2. Use the 'mysqlpump' command to create a backup of your database. Here's the basic syntax:

```
mysqlpump --user=username --password=password --host=hostname --databases
    dbname > backup.sql
```

Replace 'username', 'password', 'hostname', and 'dbname' with the appropriate values for your MySQL server. This command will create a backup of the 'dbname' database and save it to a file named 'backup.sql'.

3. By default, 'mysqlpump' creates a single-threaded backup. However, you can increase the number of threads to make the backup process faster. Here's an example command that uses four threads:

```
mysqlpump --user=username --password=password --host=hostname --databases
    dbname --parallel=4 > backup.sql
```

The '–parallel' flag specifies the number of threads to use for the backup process.

4. If you have multiple databases that you want to back up, you can use a wildcard character to specify all databases. Here's an example command that backs up all databases on the server:

```
mysqlpump --user=username --password=password --host=hostname --databases '
    *' > backup.sql
```

5. If you want to back up only certain tables within a database, you can specify them using the '–tables' flag. Here's an example command that backs up only two tables within the 'dbname' database:

```
mysqlpump --user=username --password=password --host=hostname --databases
    dbname --tables table1 table2 > backup.sql
```

6. Finally, if you want to compress the backup file to save disk space, you can pipe the output of 'mysqlpump' to a compression tool like 'gzip'. Here's an example command that creates a compressed backup:

```
mysqlpump --user=username --password=password --host=hostname --databases
    dbname | gzip > backup.sql.gz
```

That's it! By following these steps, you can create efficient and parallelized backups of your MySQL databases using the 'mysqlpump' utility.

5.16 Can you explain the role of the MySQL Thread Pool in handling high concurrency scenarios, and how do you configure it for optimal performance?

MySQL Thread Pool is a plugin that allows MySQL server to handle high-concurrency scenarios more efficiently. It works by creating multiple worker threads that can handle incoming client connections concurrently. These worker threads are pre-initialized and maintained in a pool, and are reused for handling future connection requests. This approach avoids the overhead of creating and destroying threads for each connection, which can significantly improve performance under heavy loads.

The Thread Pool plugin provides two main configuration parameters:

1. **thread_pool_size**: This parameter sets the maximum number of worker threads that can be created in the pool. The optimal value for this setting depends on the number of concurrent connections that the server receives, as well as the available system resources. A good rule of thumb is to set it to a value slightly higher than the maximum number of simultaneous connections, but not too high as to consume too much memory and CPU resources.

2. **thread_pool_stall_limit**: This parameter defines the maximum number of connection requests that can be waiting in the queue before the server starts blocking new connections. This is useful to prevent the server from becoming overloaded and to avoid exhausting resources. A value of 0 disables the queue limit, which means that the server can accept an unlimited number of connections even if it cannot handle them all.

Here is an example configuration to optimize the MySQL Thread Pool performance for handling high concurrency scenarios:

```
[mysqld]
# Enable Thread Pool plugin
plugin-load-add = thread_pool.so
# Set the maximum number of worker threads to 100
thread_pool_size = 100
# Set the maximum number of stalled connections to 50
thread_pool_stall_limit = 50
# Set the thread_pool_high_priority_mode to ON to prioritize connections with
      high priority flag set
thread_pool_high_priority_mode = ON
# Set the thread_pool_prio_kickup_timer to 500ms to quickly promote
      connections with high workload
thread_pool_prio_kickup_timer = 500ms
```

The above configuration enables the Thread Pool Plugin, sets the maximum number of worker threads to 100, and sets a limit of 50 waiting connections in the queue. It also enables the high priority mode which gives higher priority to connections with the high priority flag set. Finally, it sets a quick promotion timer of 500ms to fast-track the connection with heavy workloads.

In conclusion, configuring the MySQL Thread Pool can be a powerful tool for optimizing performance in high-concurrency scenarios. Adequate configuration is essential to avoid performance problems such as thread starvation or excessive resource consumption, and should be based on the specific workload characteristics of your MySQL server.

5.17 What are the best practices for managing high availability in a MySQL environment using technologies like MySQL Cluster, Galera Cluster, or Orchestrator?

Managing high availability in a MySQL environment is crucial for maintaining the availability of the database and ensuring that it meets the demands of the applications that rely on it. The following are best practices for managing high availability in a MySQL environment using technologies like MySQL Cluster, Galera Cluster, or Orchestrator.

1. Replication

Replication is the process of copying data from one MySQL server to another. Replication is useful for creating backups, load balancing, and high availability. Setting up asynchronous replication is relatively easy, and can help contribute to the high availability of MySQL environments. It is important to monitor the replication status, and ensure that there is no lag in data replication between the master and slave servers.

2. MySQL Cluster

MySQL Cluster is a distributed, shared-nothing database cluster. It consists of multiple nodes that work together to provide high availability, fault tolerance, and scalability. MySQL Cluster uses synchronous replication to ensure that there is no data loss. The cluster can survive individual node or hardware failure, and continue to operate without any downtime. It is important to use the correct configurations and settings for MySQL Cluster to ensure optimal performance and high availability.

3. Galera Cluster

Galera Cluster is a synchronous multi-master cluster that uses the Galera Replication Plugin to keep multiple MySQL instances in sync. Galera Cluster ensures that all active nodes have the same set of data at any given point in time. This technology is best suited for READ/WRITE intensive workloads.

4. Orchestrator

Orchestrator is a MySQL replication management and high-availability tool. It automates failovers by detecting and repairing replication problems. It can monitor replication status, issue alerts, manage failovers, and perform maintenance tasks on MySQL servers. Orchestrator adds value to the MySQL topology by automating the detection of replication issues and resolving them quickly.

5. Scalability

When scaling MySQL, it is crucial to ensure that the scaling does not impact high availability. Sharding the database can help with scalability, but it should be done carefully to ensure that it does not compromise availability. Load balancers can help distribute traffic evenly to the servers and improve the response time of the system.

In conclusion, managing high availability in a MySQL environment is not a simple task. Technologies like MySQL Cluster, Galera Cluster, and Orchestrator can help provide a reliable, high-performance, and high-availability MySQL environment. Proper configuration, monitoring, and maintenance of these technologies can help ensure that the MySQL environment is always available and reliable to support demanding applications.

5.18 How do you handle disaster recovery in a MySQL environment, and what are the key considerations when designing a recovery plan?

Disaster recovery planning is a crucial activity for any organization that manages complex information technology infrastructure, including a MySQL environment. A well-designed disaster recovery plan can mitigate the impact of adverse events on the availability of MySQL databases and ensure the continuity of critical business operations. In this answer, we will discuss the key considerations for designing a recovery plan in a MySQL environment and highlight some of the best practices for handling disasters.

First and foremost, the recovery plan should start with a comprehensive inventory of all the MySQL servers, databases, and applications that require protection. This inventory must include detailed information on the hardware, software, network topology, security protocols, and data volumes to help the disaster recovery team assess the impact of a disaster and develop an appropriate action plan. This inventory should be updated regularly to reflect any changes in the environment.

Next, the recovery plan should define the recovery objectives, including recovery time objectives (RTOs) and recovery point objectives (RPOs). The RTO is the maximum time that it takes to restore the service to the user after a disaster, while the RPO is the maximum age of the data that can be lost in the recovery process. The recovery team must prioritize the applications and data based on their criticality and define the RTOs and RPOs accordingly. For example, a highly critical transactional database may require an RTO of minutes and an RPO of seconds, whereas a less important reporting database may have an RTO of hours and an RPO of one day.

Once the recovery objectives are defined, the recovery plan should specify the procedures for backup and recovery operations. The procedures should cover the entire lifecycle of the data, including backup, archiving, replication, restore, and validation. The recovery team should use multiple types of backups, including full backups, differential backups, and incremental backups, to reduce the risk of data loss and minimize the recovery time. They should also test the backups regularly to ensure their integrity and availability.

The recovery plan should also address the network and infrastructure dependencies that can affect the recovery process. This includes the identification of the dependencies between the MySQL servers, the application servers, the storage systems, and the network components. The plan should also define the communication and escalation channels between the recovery team members, the IT staff, and the management to ensure the timely response and resolution of the disaster.

In addition to the technical aspects, the recovery plan should also consider the human factors, such as the skills, roles, and responsibilities of the recovery team members. The plan should identify the required skills and expertise for each team member and ensure that they have the necessary training and resources to execute their tasks. The plan should also define the roles and responsibilities of the recovery team members, including the team leader, the backup administrator, the database administrator, the network administrator, and the application administrator.

In summary, disaster recovery planning in a MySQL environment requires a comprehensive approach that covers the technical, network, and human factors of the recovery process. The recovery plan should start with a comprehensive inventory of the environment and define the recovery objectives, procedures, dependencies, and roles. The team should use multiple types of backups to minimize the data loss and ensure the availability of the backups. Finally, the recovery plan should be tested regularly and updated to reflect any changes in the environment.

5.19 What are the challenges and best practices for scaling MySQL in a containerized environment using technologies like Docker and Kubernetes?

Scaling MySQL in a containerized environment can present a number of challenges, but there are best practices and solutions that can help to mitigate these issues.

Some of the challenges of scaling MySQL in a containerized environment include:

1. Persistent data storage: When running MySQL in a container, the data is stored in the container's file system, which is not persistent. This means that if the container is deleted or recreated, the data will be lost. To address this, external storage solutions like network file systems (NFS) or cloud-based storage can be used to provide persistent storage for MySQL data.

2. Network latency: Running MySQL in a container can introduce network latency, as requests must be routed through the container's network stack. This can lead to slower database performance and increased query response times. Using a container orchestration platform like Kubernetes can help to address this by optimizing network routing and load balancing.

3. Database replication: To ensure high availability and scalability, it is common to use database replication with MySQL. However, running multiple MySQL containers can introduce challenges for replication, as each container must be configured with its own replication settings. Using a configuration management tool like Ansible or Chef can help to automate the process of configuring replication, ensuring consistency across containers.

4. Resource allocation: Running multiple MySQL containers on the same host can lead to resource contention and potential performance issues. To address this, it is important to carefully allocate resources like CPUs and memory to each container to ensure optimal performance.

Some best practices for scaling MySQL in a containerized environment include:

1. Designing for scalability: When designing MySQL containers, it is important to consider scalability from the outset. This means designing containers that are easily replica table and can be scaled horizontally to meet increased demand.

2. Using container orchestration: A container orchestration platform like Kubernetes can help to automate many of the tasks associated with scaling MySQL containers, including load balancing and replication configuration.

3. Optimizing resource usage: Careful resource allocation is critical for scaling MySQL containers. Resource usage should be monitored closely, and containers should be adjusted as needed to optimize resource utilization.

4. Using a container-specific monitoring solution: Monitoring MySQL performance in a containerized environment requires a different approach than traditional monitoring solutions. Using a container-specific monitoring solution like Prometheus can help to provide insights into container performance and resource usage.

Overall, scaling MySQL in a containerized environment using technologies like Docker and Kubernetes requires careful planning and execution. By following best practices and addressing the challenges listed above, organizations can successfully scale their MySQL databases in containerized environments.

5.20 How do you implement real-time data integration and synchronization between MySQL and other databases or data warehouses?

Real-time data integration and synchronization between MySQL and other databases or data warehouses can be achieved using different techniques and tools. In this answer, we will discuss some of the main approaches to implement this kind of integration.

Change data capture (CDC) approach

CDC is a popular technique used to replicate changes made to a database in real-time. It involves capturing changes from the source database and forwarding them to the target database. Typically, CDC works by reading transaction logs or other forms of change data from the source database and then applying those changes to the target database. CDC has many use cases ranging from reporting, backup, ETL to real-time data synchronization.

Here are the basic steps to implement a CDC approach for real-time data integration and synchronization between MySQL and another database:

1. Identify the source and target databases: In this case, the source database is MySQL, and the target database could be any other database or data warehouse such as Oracle, SQL Server, or Redshift.

2. Choose a CDC tool: There are many CDC tools available in the market such as Debezium, Attunity, and Kafka Connect. These tools differ in terms of ease of use, performance, and features.

3. Configure the CDC tool: You need to configure the CDC tool to read change data from MySQL and forward it to the target database. The configuration involves specifying the source database, target database, schema mapping, and transformation rules.

4. Monitor the CDC process: It is essential to monitor the CDC process to ensure that it is working correctly. You should monitor the logs, errors, and performance metrics.

Replication approach

Replication is another technique used to synchronize data between databases, including MySQL. Replication works by copying the changes from the source database to the target database, either in real-time or batch mode. MySQL has built-in replication capabilities that allow you to replicate data to other MySQL instances or to other databases such as Oracle or SQL Server.

Here are the basic steps to implement a replication approach for real-time data integration and synchronization between MySQL and another database:

1. Identify the source and target databases: In this case, the source database is MySQL, and the target database could be any other database or data warehouse such as Oracle, SQL Server, or Redshift.

2. Choose a replication method: MySQL supports different replication methods such as statement-based replication and row-based replication. The choice of replication method depends on the type of data you want to replicate and the performance requirements.

3. Configure MySQL replication: You need to configure MySQL replication by setting up a master-slave relationship between the source and target databases. This involves configuring the master and slave MySQL instances, setting up replication users and permissions, and configuring the replication parameters.

4. Monitor the replication process: It is essential to monitor the replication process to ensure that it is working correctly. You should monitor the replication logs, errors, and performance metrics.

ETL approach

ETL (extract, transform, and load) is a traditional approach used to extract data from a source database, transform it into a format suitable for the target database, and load it into the target database. ETL is typically used for batch processing, but it can be adapted to support real-time data integration and synchronization by using tools such as Apache Kafka, Apache Spark, or AWS Kinesis.

Here are the basic steps to implement an ETL approach for real-time data integration and synchronization between MySQL and another database:

1. Identify the source and target databases: In this case, the source database is MySQL, and the target database could be any other database or data warehouse such as Oracle, SQL Server, or Redshift.

2. Choose an ETL tool: There are many ETL tools available in the market such as Apache Kafka, Apache Spark, and AWS Kinesis. These tools differ in terms of ease of use, performance, and features.

3. Configure the ETL tool: You need to configure the ETL tool to read data from MySQL, transform it into a format suitable for the target database, and load it into the target database. The configuration involves specifying the source database, target database, transformation rules, and data flow.

4. Monitor the ETL process: It is essential to monitor the ETL process to ensure that it is working correctly. You should monitor the logs, errors, and performance metrics.

In conclusion, real-time data integration and synchronization between MySQL and other databases or data warehouses can be achieved using different approaches, including CDC, replication, and ETL. The choice of approach depends on factors such as data volume, performance requirements, and the complexity of the data transformation.

Chapter 6

Guru

6.1 Can you discuss the internals of the InnoDB storage engine, including its file structure, transaction handling, and locking mechanisms?

The InnoDB storage engine is a transactional engine that provides ACID (Atomicity, Consistency, Isolation, and Durability) compliance. It is the default engine used by MySQL since version 5.5.

File Structure:

InnoDB stores data and indexes in tablespace files (*.ibd) located in the data directory. The data dictionary and other metadata are stored in system tablespaces (ibdata files) also located in the data directory.

InnoDB uses a multi-versioning scheme to store the data in its tablespace files. This means that for each row modification, a new version is created keeping the old version intact. This is done to support read consistency and transaction isolation levels.

Transaction Handling:

InnoDB provides full ACID compliance by supporting transactions. In a transactional system, a set of SQL statements is considered a single logical unit of work. Either all the statements in the set are executed successfully, or the entire transaction is rolled back. This ensures data integrity and consistency.

InnoDB uses a technique called "change buffering" to improve transaction throughput. Change buffering groups together small changes made to a page and writes them in a batch to disk later. This reduces the number of disk write operations and makes the transactional process more efficient.

Locking Mechanisms:

InnoDB uses a combination of shared and exclusive locks to maintain data consistency and isolation. The lock types can be applied at different granularities, such as table-level, row-level, or even at the page-level.

InnoDB also provides a feature called "locking reads" that allows transactions to acquire shared locks on rows they read. This ensures that other transactions cannot modify the same rows concurrently.

InnoDB also has the capability to allow multiple transactions to access the same row concurrently, depending on the isolation level. For example, at the default isolation level of REPEATABLE READ, a single transaction can hold shared locks on various rows, while another transaction can read but not modify those same rows.

In summary, the InnoDB storage engine has a robust file structure that supports multi-versioning, a transaction handling mechanism that provides ACID compliance, and locking mechanisms that ensure data consistency and isolation.

6.2 How do you use advanced techniques like materialized views, covering indexes, and query hints to optimize complex MySQL queries in large-scale applications?

When dealing with large-scale applications, optimizing MySQL queries becomes crucial for reducing response times and ensuring efficient use of resources. Here are some advanced techniques that can help optimize complex MySQL queries:

Materialized Views
Materialized views are precomputed tables that store the results of a query. They are updated periodically or on-demand and are used to improve the performance of complex queries by reducing the need for calculations during execution.

To create a materialized view in MySQL, we first create the base query that defines the results we want to cache. Then we use the 'CREATE MATERIALIZED VIEW' statement to create a new table that stores the results of the query. Finally, we use the 'REFRESH MATERIALIZED VIEW' statement to update the view when needed.

For example, let's say we have a complex query that joins multiple tables and performs calculations:

```
SELECT a.id, SUM(b.amount * c.rate) as total
FROM table_a a
JOIN table_b b ON a.id = b.a_id
JOIN table_c c ON b.c_id = c.id
WHERE a.date BETWEEN '2021-01-01' AND '2021-12-31'
GROUP BY a.id
```

We can create a materialized view of this query as follows:

```
CREATE MATERIALIZED VIEW mv_totals AS
SELECT a.id, SUM(b.amount * c.rate) as total
FROM table_a a
JOIN table_b b ON a.id = b.a_id
JOIN table_c c ON b.c_id = c.id
GROUP BY a.id
```

And then refresh the view periodically or on-demand using:

```
REFRESH MATERIALIZED VIEW mv_totals
```

Now, we can query the materialized view instead of the original query:

```
SELECT * FROM mv_totals WHERE date BETWEEN '2021-01-01' AND '2021-12-31'
```

This can significantly reduce the response time of our queries as the results are precomputed and stored in the materialized view.

Covering Indexes

Covering indexes are indexes that contain all the columns needed to satisfy a query. They allow MySQL to retrieve the required data directly from the index, avoiding the need to access the underlying table.

For example, let's consider the following query:

```
SELECT name, age FROM users WHERE gender = 'Male' AND age BETWEEN 25 AND 40
```

We can create a covering index on the 'gender' and 'age' columns, as well as the 'name' and 'age' columns, as follows:

```
CREATE INDEX idx_gender_age ON users (gender, age, name)
```

Now, when we execute the query, MySQL can use the covering index to satisfy the query without accessing the underlying table:

```
EXPLAIN SELECT name, age FROM users WHERE gender = 'Male' AND age BETWEEN 25
    AND 40

id select_type table partitions type possible_keys key       key_len ref
    rows   filtered  Extra
1   SIMPLE    users NULL       ref    idx_gender_age idx_gender_age 4 const
    100    50.00     Using index condition
```

The 'type' column in the 'EXPLAIN' output shows that MySQL is using the covering index to satisfy the query.

Query Hints

Query hints are special comments that we can add to our queries to provide additional information to MySQL's query optimizer. They can help MySQL choose the most efficient query execution plan, especially when dealing with complex queries.

For example, let's say we have a query that joins multiple tables:

```
SELECT *
FROM table_a a
JOIN table_b b ON a.id = b.a_id
JOIN table_c c ON b.c_id = c.id
WHERE a.date BETWEEN '2021-01-01' AND '2021-12-31'
```

We can provide a hint that tells MySQL to use a specific join order:

```
SELECT /*+ JOIN_ORDER(a b c) */ *
FROM table_a a
JOIN table_b b ON a.id = b.a_id
JOIN table_c c ON b.c_id = c.id
WHERE a.date BETWEEN '2021-01-01' AND '2021-12-31'
```

The '/*+ JOIN_ORDER(a b c) */' hint tells MySQL to join the tables in the order 'a', 'b', and 'c'. This can be useful when MySQL's query optimizer chooses a suboptimal join order.

In conclusion, materialized views, covering indexes, and query hints are all powerful techniques that can help optimize complex MySQL queries in large-scale applications. By precomputing results, avoiding table access, and providing additional information to the query optimizer, we can significantly reduce query response times and improve overall performance.

6.3 What are the trade-offs between using read replicas, sharding, and distributed databases when designing a high-performance and scalable MySQL architecture?

When designing a high-performance and scalable MySQL architecture, there are several options available, including the use of read replicas, sharding, and distributed databases. Each option has its advantages and disadvantages, and choosing the right option depends on several factors, such as the nature of the application workload, the amount of data to be stored and processed, and the desired level of scalability and availability. In this answer, we will discuss the trade-offs of each option and when to use them.

Read Replicas

Read replicas are copies of the primary database that are used to serve read traffic, offloading read queries from the main database and reducing its load. Read replicas are typically used in applications with a high read-to-write ratio, in which read traffic is a bottleneck. One advantage of read replicas is that they are easy to set up and require no application-level changes. Additionally, read replicas can provide high availability and failover support, as they can automatically take over if the primary database fails.

However, read replicas also have some limitations. First, they are not suitable for applications with high write traffic since writes still need to go to the primary database, leading to write contention and decreased performance. Second, read replicas can introduce eventual consistency issues since there may be a delay between the time a write is made to the primary database and the time it is replicated to the read replica, which can lead to data inconsistencies if read queries are served from the replicas instead of the primary database.

Sharding

Sharding is a technique in which a large dataset is partitioned across multiple smaller databases called shards, each responsible for storing and processing a subset of the data. Sharding is typically used in applications with high write traffic since it distributes the write load across multiple databases, improving the write throughput and reducing write contention. Additionally, sharding can provide improved scalability since new shards can be added as the dataset grows.

However, sharding also has some disadvantages. First, it is more complex to set up and maintain compared to read replicas since the application needs to be aware of the sharding scheme and route queries to the appropriate shard. Second, sharding can lead to increased data inconsistency if the sharding scheme is not well-designed, and some shards receive more write traffic than others, leading to unbalanced data distribution.

Distributed Databases

Distributed databases are databases that are spread across multiple nodes in a network, providing high availability and fault tolerance. Distributed databases can be used for both read and write traffic, and they can provide linear scalability as new nodes are added to the network. Additionally, distributed databases can provide high performance since data can be accessed from nodes that are closer to the application users.

However, distributed databases also have some limitations. First, they are more complex to set up and maintain compared to read replicas and sharding, and they require a distributed consensus protocol to ensure data consistency and availability. Second, distributed databases can incur higher latency due to the need to communicate with multiple nodes in the network, which can impact the application's performance.

In conclusion, choosing the right option for designing a high-performance and scalable MySQL architecture depends on various factors, including the application workload, data size, and desired level of scalability and availability. Read replicas are suitable for applications that have high read-to-write ratios, and sharding is appropriate for applications with high write traffic. Finally, distributed databases provide high availability and scalability for both read and write traffic, but they are more complex to set up and maintain.

6.4 How do you evaluate and choose the most suitable MySQL storage engine for a specific use case, considering factors like performance, concurrency, and data integrity?

There are multiple factors you should consider when choosing a MySQL storage engine for a specific use case. In this answer, we will focus on three main factors: performance, concurrency, and data integrity.

Performance

When it comes to performance, the type of workload that the storage engine is going to receive should be the main consideration. Some storage engines, such as MyISAM, are optimized for read-heavy workloads, while others, such as InnoDB or TokuDB, can be better suited for write-heavy workloads.

MyISAM

MyISAM is a storage engine that is optimized for read operations. It's very fast for read-intensive workloads or when there is mostly static data in the database. It doesn't support transactions or foreign keys, so it's not recommended for applications that require a high level of data integrity or security. Also, since it lacks support for row-level locking, it can have issues with concurrency control on a high number of writes.

InnoDB

InnoDB is a storage engine that is optimized for write-intensive workloads. It has support for transactions, foreign keys, and row-level locking, which make it a good choice for applications that require a high level of data integrity and security. It's slower than MyISAM for read-intensive workloads, but it scales better with a high number of concurrent writes.

TokuDB

TokuDB is a storage engine that is optimized for both read and write workloads. It's well suited for applications that need to store a large volume of data and that require fast inserts, updates, and reads. It has support for transactions and compression, which can help to reduce storage costs. TokuDB performs well on write-heavy workloads thanks to its efficient write-optimized storage engine that clusters small writes together before flushing them to disk.

Concurrency

Concurrency is an important factor to consider when choosing a storage engine. Concurrency refers to the ability of the storage engine to handle multiple users accessing the database at the same time. A storage engine with good concurrency controls should be chosen when the application is expected to have a high number of concurrent users.

MyISAM

MyISAM has table-level locking, which means that when one user is writing to a table, other users can't access it. This can cause contention and delays in a high-concurrency environment, making it not suitable for concurrent write operations. In contrast, multiple read operations to the same table can be executed simultaneously.

InnoDB

InnoDB supports row-level locking, which makes it more efficient for concurrent updates and reads. As a result, performance doesn't deteriorate significantly in high-concurrency environments. InnoDB uses a multi-versioning concurrency control (MVCC) model that allows for high levels of concurrent read and write operations.

TokuDB

TokuDB provides good concurrency thanks to its efficient write-optimized storage engine that clusters small writes together before flushing them to disk.

Data Integrity

Data integrity refers to the accuracy and consistency of data stored in a database. It's important to choose a storage engine that can ensure data integrity, especially if the application handles sensitive data.

MyISAM

MyISAM doesn't support transactions or foreign keys, which can lead to data inconsistencies in case of failures, power outages, or crashes. It's not recommended for applications that require a high level of data integrity or security.

InnoDB

InnoDB supports transactions and foreign keys, which make it more reliable for data integrity. InnoDB provides support for 'ACID (Atomicity, Consistency, Isolation, Durability)' transactions, which ensure that the data is always in a consistent state, even in case of failures.

TokuDB

TokuDB supports transactions, which ensure operations are performed atomically, maximizing the consistency of the data. In addition, TokuDB provides automatic compression of data on writes, reducing the storage costs prerequisite. This also reduces write I/O and enhances durability, as it reduces the size of data written to disk.

In conclusion, choosing the most suitable MySQL storage engine for a specific use case requires a deep understanding of the workload patterns, the concurrency levels, and the data integrity requirements of an application. This allows us to select the storage engine that provides the best performance and reliability, fulfilling the requirements of the application.

6.5   How do you implement real-time monitoring and alerting for critical MySQL performance and availability metrics, using custom tools or third-party solutions?

Real-time monitoring and alerting for critical MySQL performance and availability metrics is crucial for ensuring the optimal performance, availability, and reliability of MySQL databases. There are several custom tools and third-party solutions available for this purpose. In this answer, I will discuss some of the popular options for implementing real-time monitoring and alerting for critical MySQL performance and availability metrics.

1. MySQL Enterprise Monitor:
MySQL Enterprise Monitor is one of the popular third-party solutions for real-time monitoring and alerting of critical MySQL performance and availability metrics. It is a comprehensive tool that provides a graphical user interface for monitoring and alerting on MySQL performance issues, including bottlenecks, slow queries, replication lag, and more. The tool provides real-time visibility into the MySQL database's performance and health status, enabling efficient performance tuning and optimization.

MySQL Enterprise Monitor comes with a built-in alerting system that allows users to set up preconfigured alerts or customize alerts based on their specific needs. The alerting system supports a wide range of notification channels, including email, SMS, and PagerDuty.

MySQL Enterprise Monitor also provides historical analysis and reporting capabilities, enabling users to identify performance trends and track key performance metrics over time.

2. Nagios:
Nagios is a popular open-source monitoring tool that supports monitoring of MySQL databases. It is a customizable tool that can be extended with plugins to monitor a wide range of metrics, including database connections, queries per second, replication lag, and more.

Nagios has a flexible alerting system that can be configured to send notifications via email, SMS, or other means when monitored metrics exceed predefined thresholds. Nagios also supports historical reporting and analysis, enabling users to track performance trends over time.

3. Zabbix:
Zabbix is another open-source monitoring solution that can be used to monitor MySQL performance and availability metrics. It provides real-time monitoring of critical metrics such as database connections, queries per second, replication lag, and more.

Zabbix has a comprehensive alerting system that supports multiple notification channels, including email, SMS, and Slack. Users can set up custom alerting rules based on their specific needs.

Zabbix also provides historical analysis and reporting capabilities, enabling users to track metrics over time and identify performance trends.

4. InfluxDB and Grafana:
InfluxDB is a time-series database that can be used to store and analyze metrics from MySQL databases. Grafana is an open-source monitoring and visualization platform that can be used to create custom dashboards and visualize metric data stored in InfluxDB.

Together, InfluxDB and Grafana can be used to implement real-time monitoring and alerting for critical MySQL performance and availability metrics. Users can configure InfluxDB to store and handle metric data from MySQL databases, while Grafana can be used to visualize the data through custom dashboards. Both tools support alerting based on predefined thresholds, enabling users to receive notifications when critical metrics exceed predefined thresholds.

In conclusion, real-time monitoring and alerting for critical MySQL performance and availability metrics can be implemented using custom tools, third-party solutions or their combination. The right option depends on the specifics of the environment and the required features.

6.6 What are some advanced techniques for MySQL query optimization, including rewriting suboptimal queries, using partial or filtered indexes, and leveraging optimizer hints?

MySQL query optimization is vital to improve the database's performance and reduce query time, especially when working with large amounts of data. In this answer, I will discuss some advanced techniques for MySQL query optimization.

1. Rewriting suboptimal queries:

Suboptimal queries are those that can be written in a more efficient way. One common technique is to rewrite a subquery using a join. For example, suppose we have two tables, "products" and "orders," and we want to find the products that have not been ordered yet. One possible query is:

```
SELECT *
FROM products
WHERE id NOT IN (
  SELECT product_id
  FROM orders
)
```

However, this query can be slow if the "orders" table is large. A better alternative is to use a left join:

```
SELECT products.*
FROM products
LEFT JOIN orders ON products.id = orders.product_id
WHERE orders.product_id IS NULL
```

This query performs better because the left join eliminates the need for a subquery, and the WHERE clause filters out the products with non-null order IDs. It's always worth experimenting with different query styles to see which performs best.

2. Using partial or filtered indexes:

Indexes are essential for querying large tables efficiently. MySQL supports partial and filtered indexes, which can significantly improve query performance in some cases. A partial index is an index that covers only a subset of the rows in a table, while a filtered index covers only those rows that satisfy a particular condition.

Suppose we have a table "users" with millions of rows, and we often query for users with a particular flag set:

```
SELECT *
FROM users
WHERE is_active = 1
```

Instead of creating an index on the "is_active" column, which would be inefficient due to its low cardinality, we can create a filtered index:

```
CREATE INDEX idx_active_users ON users (id) WHERE is_active = 1;
```

This index covers only the active users, making queries that filter by the "is_active" flag much faster.

3. Leveraging optimizer hints:

MySQL provides several optimizer hints that let us provide additional information to the query optimizer to help it choose a more optimal execution plan. Some useful hints include:

- USE INDEX: Forces the optimizer to use a specific index when executing a query, even if it's not the optimal index according to its cost-based model.

- IGNORE INDEX: Forces the optimizer to ignore a specific index when executing a query.

- FORCE INDEX: Forces the optimizer to choose a specific index when executing a query, even if it's not the optimal index according to its cost-based model.

For example, suppose we have a table "customers" with two indexes, one on the "last_name" column and one on the "first_name" column. If we often query by both columns, we can use the USE INDEX hint to force the optimizer to use the composite index:

```
SELECT *
FROM customers USE INDEX (last_name, first_name)
WHERE last_name = 'Doe' AND first_name = 'John'
```

This query will perform faster than if we let the optimizer choose either the "last_name" or "first_name" index separately.

In conclusion, these techniques are only a few of many advanced techniques that can be used for MySQL Query Optimization. MySQL query optimization requires a lot of experimentation, and understanding the database schema and querying pattern before deciding which technique to use. There is no one size fits all solution, but by following good practices and experimenting with different methods, we can have a competitive solution.

6.7   Can you discuss the differences between synchronous, asynchronous, and group replication in MySQL, and their implications for data consistency, performance, and fault tolerance?

Synchronous Replication:

Synchronous replication is a type of replication in which the primary database waits for confirmation from all of the replicas before committing a transaction. This means that a transaction is not considered complete until all replicas have received the transaction and acknowledge its success. It ensures strong data consistency but can lead to slower performance due to the extra overhead of waiting for all replicas to respond.

Synchronous replication is useful in scenarios where it's critical that all replicas have the same data at all times, such as in financial institutions, where data consistency is paramount. Here is an example of synchronous replication:

```
CHANGE MASTER TO MASTER_HOST='primary',
    MASTER_USER='replica',
```

```
MASTER_PASSWORD='replica_password',
MASTER_PORT=3306,
MASTER_LOG_FILE='filename',
MASTER_LOG_POS=position;
```

Asynchronous Replication:

Asynchronous replication, on the other hand, is a type of replication in which the primary database commits a transaction without waiting for confirmation from all of the replicas. This means that a transaction can be considered complete on the primary database even if some or all replicas have not yet received the transaction. It's faster than synchronous replication, but it may lead to data inconsistencies.

Asynchronous replication is commonly used in scenarios where performance is critical, and data consistency can be sacrificed slightly since the data eventually gets synchronized across all replicas. Here's an example of asynchronous replication:

```
CHANGE MASTER TO MASTER_HOST='primary',
    MASTER_USER='replica',
    MASTER_PASSWORD='replica_password',
    MASTER_PORT=3306,
    MASTER_LOG_FILE='filename',
    MASTER_LOG_POS=position;
```

Group Replication:

Group replication is a type of synchronous replication that provides fault tolerance and high availability. It uses a group of servers acting together to provide a single replicated database service. Each server in the group receives a transaction and votes on whether to commit the transaction. If a server fails, another server takes over, and the group continues to operate normally.

Group replication is useful in scenarios where high availability and fault tolerance are necessary, such as in e-commerce websites. Here's an example of group replication:

```
SET GLOBAL group_replication_bootstrap_group=OFF;
START GROUP_REPLICATION;
```

Implications for Data Consistency, Performance, and Fault Tolerance:

- Data Consistency:

Synchronous replication provides the strongest data consistency since it waits for all replicas to confirm a transaction before committing it. Asynchronous replication sacrifices some consistency for the sake of performance. Group replication provides strong consistency while also providing fault tolerance and high availability.

- Performance:

Synchronous replication usually leads to slower performance because it requires confirmation from all replicas before committing a transaction. Asynchronous replication is faster since it doesn't require confirmation from all replicas. Group replication can be slower than asynchronous replication but is still relatively fast while also providing fault tolerance and high availability.

- Fault Tolerance:

Synchronous and group replication provides fault tolerance, ensuring that any transaction that is committed is replicated across all replicas. Asynchronous replication may lead to data inconsistencies and may not provide fault tolerance.

In conclusion, choosing the right replication method for your MySQL database depends on the use case. For scenarios where data consistency is paramount, synchronous replication is the best option. For scenarios where performance is critical, and data consistency can be compromised slightly, asynchronous replication may be the right option. And for scenarios where both data consistency and fault tolerance are necessary, group replication is the most suitable option.

6.8   How do you ensure the security of MySQL deployments in compliance with industry standards and regulations like GDPR, HIPAA, and PCI DSS?

Securing a MySQL deployment is crucial due to databases' sensitivity and the potential damage data breaches can cause. In the following sections, I will discuss some measures that can be taken to ensure the security of MySQL databases in compliance with industry standards and regulations such as GDPR, HIPAA, and PCI DSS.

1. Encryption

Data encryption is crucial to protect data from unauthorized access, especially if the data is transmitted over the internet or stored on portable devices. MySQL offers several encryption options, including SSL/TLS encryption for securing connections to the database and data-at-rest encryption using third-party tools like VeraCrypt or BitLocker. Encryption ensures that the data is only accessible by authorized users and can be decrypted only with the appropriate keys.

2. Access control

Access control is an essential factor in securing a MySQL database. Ensuring that user accounts have strong passwords and limiting access based on the principle of least privilege is crucial. Principle of least privilege means giving users or processes only the permissions they need to perform their tasks and nothing more. MySQL provides various user authentication mechanisms, including password authentication and external authentication through plugins or PAM (Pluggable Authentication Module).

3. Auditing

Auditing, also known as logging, helps to track and monitor activities on the database, including unsuccessful login attempts, connection attempts, and data changes. MySQL supports various logging options, including general query log, slow query log, and error log. It is also essential to ensure that logs are stored in a secure location and only accessible by authorized personnel.

4. Backup and recovery

Regular backups of a MySQL database are essential to ensure data
recovery in case of accidental deletion, corruption, or data breaches.
Backups can be stored on a different server, in cloud storage, or on
removable media, depending on the organization's needs. Organizations must ensure that backups are encrypted or stored securely to
prevent unauthorized access.

5. Security patches and updates

MySQL is an actively developed database, which means there are regular security patches and updates released to address security vulnerabilities. Organizations must ensure that their MySQL deployment is
up-to-date and that security patches are applied regularly to reduce
the risk of data breaches.

In conclusion, securing a MySQL database is crucial to comply with
industry standards and regulations like GDPR, HIPAA, and PCI
DSS. It involves a combination of measures, including encryption,
access control, auditing, backup and recovery, and regular security
patches and updates. Organizations must ensure that each measure
they take is implemented appropriately and that all measures work
together to provide a robust and comprehensive security solution.

6.9   How do you plan and execute the migration of large-scale MySQL deployments to cloud-based solutions like Amazon RDS, Google Cloud SQL, or Azure Database for MySQL?

Migrating a large-scale MySQL deployment to a cloud-based solution
can be a challenging task that requires careful planning and execution.
The following steps can help to ensure a successful migration:

1. **Assess the current deployment**: Start by assessing the current

deployment to determine the size and complexity of the database environment. This will help to identify any potential issues or challenges that may arise during the migration process. Look for the following information:

* The size of the database (in terms of data and metadata)

* Number of databases and tables, indexes, and stored procedures

* Server hardware and software configurations

* Growth over time, if any trends observed during this period.

2. **Choose the cloud-based solution**: Once you have assessed the current MySQL deployment, you need to choose a cloud-based solution that best fits your requirements. Popular choices for cloud-based MySQL deployment include Amazon RDS, Google Cloud SQL, and Azure Database for MySQL. Consider the following when deciding:

* The cost and features of each option

* The scalability of the solution

* The level of control and customization offered

* The geographic location of data centers.

3. **Create a migration plan**: After choosing the cloud-based solution, create a detailed migration plan. The plan should include the following steps:

* Determine the migration scope and plan

* Set up the target database on the cloud platform

* Prepare the source database for migration by cleaning up data and optimizing performance

* Choose a migration method: data dump and reload, replication, or online migration

* Perform the migration and validate the results

* Test the application to ensure it works correctly with the migrated database

* Plan a fallback strategy in case of issues during migration.

4. **Perform the migration**: Once you have a migration plan, it is time to execute the migration. There are several methods to migrate MySQL data, such as:

* Data dump and reload: This method involves dumping data from the source database and loading it into the target database. This method is suitable for small databases, but can be time-consuming for large databases.

* Replication: This method involves setting up replication between the source and target databases. This method can be used for large databases, but requires significant modifications to the source database.

* Online migration: This method involves using tools like AWS Database Migration Service or Cloud SQL Migration Service that can migrate the data with minimal downtime.

5. **Validate and test the migration**: After completing the migration, validate and test the migrated data to ensure that everything is working as expected. Check for the following:

* Data accuracy and completeness

* Data consistency

* Performance and scalability

* Application compatibility and functionality.

6. **Optimize the new cloud-based environment**: Once the migration is complete, you can further optimize the new environment for better performance, availability, and scalability. Some optimization strategies include:

* Monitoring and tuning the database performance

* Implementing automatic backups and disaster recovery plans

* Leveraging cloud-native services like load balancers and auto-scaling groups.

In summary, migrating a large-scale MySQL deployment to a cloud-based solution requires proper planning, choosing the right solution, executing the migration process, validation and testing, and optimization of the new environment. Proper planning, precise execution, and continuous monitoring can help ensure a smooth and successful migration.

6.10   Can you discuss advanced strategies for data partitioning in MySQL, including horizontal and vertical partitioning, as well as the challenges and benefits of each approach?

Data partitioning is the process of dividing a large database table into smaller and more manageable parts. Partitioning can improve query performance, reduce resource consumption and make maintenance activities more manageable. Partitioning strategies in MySQL can be broadly classified into two types: horizontal partitioning and vertical partitioning.

Horizontal Partitioning:

Horizontal partitioning, also known as sharding, involves horizontally splitting a large table into smaller tables or shards. Each partition contains a subset of the data, usually distinguished by a key range, a hash value or some other criteria. Horizontal partitioning is most suitable for large and frequently-used tables that cannot be efficiently indexed, or whose indexes cannot fit into memory. Benefits of horizontal partitioning include parallel queries, reduced disk seeks and less contention for resources. However, horizontal partitioning can introduce complexity and overhead, making it unsuitable for smaller databases or those with low write loads.

Vertical Partitioning:

Vertical partitioning involves splitting a table into smaller sub-tables based on their relationship to each other. For example, a table may be split into a "base" table containing only the most frequently accessed columns, and a "rest" table containing the remaining columns. Vertical partitioning can improve query performance by only retrieving the data needed to answer a particular query. It can also simplify maintenance by allowing columns to be added or dropped without affecting the entire table. However, vertical partitioning can introduce complexity when joining tables and can be less effective in reducing resource consumption than horizontal partitioning.

Hybrid Partitioning:

Hybrid partitioning involves combining horizontal and vertical partitioning to achieve better performance and more efficient use of resources. For example, a large table may be horizontally partitioned by key range, and each partition may be further vertically partitioned into sub-tables. Hybrid partitioning can be effective in reducing disk seeks and improving I/O throughput, but can be difficult to implement and maintain.

In summary, data partitioning can bring significant performance benefits to MySQL databases, but requires careful planning and implementation. Horizontal partitioning is most useful for large and frequently-used tables, while vertical partitioning is best suited for tables with a large number of columns or where only a subset of the columns are frequently accessed. Hybrid partitioning can provide the best of both worlds, but comes with added complexity and overhead.

6.11   What are some emerging trends and technologies in the database management domain that can impact the future of MySQL and its ecosystem?

The database management domain is continuously evolving, and new trends and technologies are emerging regularly. Some of the emerging trends and technologies in the database management domain that can impact the future of MySQL and its ecosystem are:

1. Big Data: The growth of data is exponential, and organizations are generating more data than ever before. Managing and analyzing large amounts of data is critical for businesses to make informed decisions. MySQL supports big data solutions by offering features like sharding and partitioning, which help in distributing data across multiple servers.

2. Cloud Computing: Cloud computing has become a common and popular way of deploying and managing applications. With cloud-based database management systems, users can easily access data from anywhere and at any time. MySQL has also introduced a cloud-based version known as MySQL Cloud Service, which offers features like scalability, performance, and security.

3. AI and Machine Learning: Artificial Intelligence (AI) and
Machine Learning (ML) are transforming the database management
domain. MySQL offers support for this trend by integrating with
AI/ML tools such as TensorFlow and PyTorch. These tools can help
with forecasting, classification, and decision-making processes, which
are particularly useful for analytics applications.

4. NoSQL: NoSQL databases are becoming increasingly popular
for handling large volumes of unstructured data. MySQL also offers
NoSQL capabilities with the JSON data type and related functions.
These features make it possible to store and query JSON documents,
making MySQL a viable NoSQL solution.

5. Blockchain Data Management: The use of blockchain technology is growing rapidly, and databases are playing a critical role.
MySQL can support blockchain applications by providing a distributed
architecture with high scalability and availability.

In conclusion, the future of MySQL and its ecosystem is likely to
be shaped by emerging trends and technologies such as big data,
cloud computing, AI/ML, NoSQL, and blockchain data management.
MySQL has already started to integrate with these technologies and
is expected to continue to evolve to meet the demands of modern
database management.

6.12 How do you assess the performance impact of new features, configurations, or infrastructure changes in a MySQL environment using benchmarking, profiling, and A/B testing techniques?

Assessing the performance impact of new features, configurations, or
infrastructure changes in a MySQL environment is crucial to ensure
that the system runs efficiently and effectively. Benchmarking, profiling, and A/B testing are essential techniques that can be used to
assess and optimize performance.

Benchmarking

Benchmarking is the process of measuring the performance of a system against a known standard or reference point. It involves running a series of tests using different workload types, sizes, and configurations to evaluate the resource utilization and response times of the system.

Types of Benchmarking

Functional Benchmarking: This type of benchmarking tests the functionality of the entire system, focusing on the performance of common tasks. It assesses the processing speeds of transactions, database queries, and other operations.

Workload/Volume Benchmarking: This type of benchmarking tests the system's performance with different workloads and volumes. It assesses the throughput capacity of the system, measuring how many transactions or queries it can handle in a given time.

Capacity Benchmarking: This type of benchmarking tests the system's capacity to handle peak loads. It evaluates the system's ability to handle maximum loads without performance degradation or failures.

Steps in Benchmarking

The following are the steps involved in benchmarking a MySQL environment:

Identify the benchmark requirements and goals, and define the workload model based on the actual workload or expected workload of the system.

Prepare the benchmark tests including a test runner program, test data, and test environment.

Execute the tests and analyze the results. The analysis should include factors such as response time, throughput, CPU usage, memory usage, disk I/O, network I/O, and database queries.

Identify the bottlenecks or performance issues, and optimize the system based on the results.

Profiling

Profiling refers to the process of identifying performance issues in a system by tracing the execution of code and analyzing the resource usage of each component. It involves collecting and analyzing data on CPU usage, memory consumption, disk I/O, and other system resources to identify the root cause of performance issues.

MySQL provides profiling tools that allow you to monitor and analyze the performance of queries and transactions. **SET PROFILING** is used to enable profiling and **SHOW PROFILE** is used to display the profiling information.

A/B Testing

A/B testing involves running two versions of an application or configuration simultaneously and comparing their performance metrics to determine which version is more effective. In MySQL, A/B testing can be done at multiple levels such as:

Operating system level: by testing different file systems, kernel parameters, network configurations, etc.

Database level: by testing different storage engines, indexing methods, replication configurations, query optimizations, etc.

Application level: by testing different code dependencies, caching mechanisms, etc.

A/B testing can be done using various tools such as Apache JMeter, MySQL Router, and ProxySQL.

In conclusion, benchmarking, profiling, and A/B testing are imperative for evaluating and optimizing the performance of a MySQL environment. By using these techniques, you can identify the root cause of performance issues and optimize the system for maximum efficiency and effectiveness.

6.13   Can you discuss the role of MySQL in hybrid and multi-cloud environments, and how to ensure seamless data integration, security, and performance across multiple platforms?

MySQL is a popular open-source relational database management system that is widely used in hybrid and multi-cloud environments due to its flexibility, scalability, and ease of integration with other technologies. In a hybrid environment, MySQL can be deployed in both on-premise and cloud-based environments, enabling organizations to leverage the benefits of both environments to optimize their IT infrastructure.

In a multi-cloud environment, MySQL can be deployed on multiple cloud platforms such as Amazon Web Services (AWS), Microsoft Azure, and Google Cloud, among others. This allows organizations to take advantage of the benefits of different cloud providers to meet their specific business needs. However, managing data across multiple environments can be complex, and organizations need to ensure seamless data integration, security, and performance across multiple platforms.

One way to ensure seamless data integration across multiple platforms is to use a cloud-based ETL (extract, transform, load) solution. ETL tools can help organizations automate the process of extracting data from different sources, transforming the data into a format that is compatible with MySQL, and loading the data into the MySQL database.

To ensure security, organizations need to implement a multi-layered security strategy, which includes network security, data encryption, access control, and monitoring. Network security can be achieved by deploying firewalls and using virtual private networks (VPNs) to secure data transmission. Data encryption can be done by using encryption technologies such as SSL or TLS to protect data when it is transmitted over the internet. Access control can be implemented by setting up user accounts with different levels of privileges to ensure that only authorized users can access data. Finally, monitoring can be done using tools such as Security Information and Event Management (SIEM) systems to detect and respond to security incidents in real-time.

Performance is another critical consideration in a multi-cloud environment. To ensure optimal performance, organizations need to optimize the MySQL database for the specific cloud platform and workload. This can be done by tuning the database parameters, optimizing the database schema, and using caching technologies such as Redis or Memcached.

In summary, MySQL can play a critical role in hybrid and multi-cloud environments, but organizations need to ensure seamless data integration, security, and performance across multiple platforms. By implementing a multi-layered security strategy, using ETL tools for data integration, and optimizing the MySQL database for the specific cloud platform and workload, organizations can achieve optimal results in their hybrid and multi-cloud deployments.

6.14   How do you troubleshoot and resolve complex MySQL performance issues that involve multiple layers of the application stack, such as code, database, and infrastructure?

When it comes to troubleshooting and resolving complex MySQL performance issues that involves multiple layers of the application stack, there is no one definitive approach. It often depends on the specific issue at hand, available resources, and the expertise of the team involved. Nevertheless, the following are the general steps to follow to troubleshoot and resolve complex MySQL performance issues that involve multiple layers of the application stack.

Step 1. Identify the symptoms: The starting point is to try to identify the symptoms of the problem. Symptoms could include slow database queries, long response times, high CPU or memory usage, low throughput, or high disk I/O. It's important to gather as much information as possible about the symptoms, including when they occur, what triggers them, and how long they last.

Step 2. Collect data: Once you have identified the symptoms, the next step is to gather data. You need to collect data from multiple sources, including the database, application code, and infrastructure. This data can include:

1. MySQL slow query logs

2. Application logs

3. System performance metrics such as CPU usage, memory usage, disk I/O and network I/O

4. Operating system and software configuration settings

Step 3. Analyze data: The next step is to analyze the collected data. This involves going through the logs, performance metrics, and configuration settings to identify patterns or anomalies.

Step 4. Narrow down the problem: Based on the analysis of the data, you need to narrow down the potential causes of the problem. This could mean identifying a single offending query, a poorly written piece of code, a misconfigured server or networking issue. While doing this, it's recommended to focus on the most impactful issues first.

Step 5. Develop a plan to address the problem: After determining the root cause of the issue, the next step is to determine the best course of action to take to address the problem. This can include rewriting queries, optimizing configuration settings, updating software versions or adding more hardware.

Step 6. Execute the plan: Finally, once you have developed a plan, it's time to execute it. It's important to carefully document all changes made to the system, as well as their results, so you can learn from the experience if a similar problem arises in the future.

In conclusion, when it comes to troubleshooting and resolving complex MySQL performance issues that involve multiple layers of the application stack, taking a systematic approach is critical. By following these steps, you can minimize downtime and optimize your MySQL-powered applications for maximum performance.

6.15   What are the best practices for automating database operations and maintenance tasks in a MySQL environment, using tools like Ansible, Puppet, or custom scripts?

Automating database operations and maintenance tasks in a MySQL environment is crucial for efficient, reliable and secure database management. Using automation tools such as Ansible, Puppet, or custom scripts can significantly reduce the effort, time and errors involved in manual operations. In this answer, I will discuss the best practices for automating database operations and maintenance tasks in a MySQL environment.

1. Use Configuration Management Tools:

Configuration Management tools such as Ansible, Chef and Puppet can be used to automate the setup and configuration of MySQL servers. These tools are easy to use, highly configurable, provide declarative syntax and make it easy to maintain MySQL servers at scale. For example, by using Ansible, database administrators can define YAML files that specify the configuration of MySQL servers, including server settings, users and roles, replication, backups, and security. Ansible then applies the configuration to the servers, ensuring consistency across the entire environment.

2. Use Backup and Recovery Automation:

Regular backups are critical to protecting MySQL databases from data loss or corruption. Performing manual backups can be time-consuming and error-prone. To ensure reliable backups and recovery, use backup and recovery automation tools such as XtraBackup or mysqldump. These tools can be scheduled and triggered automatically and can be customized to meet specific backup and recovery requirements.

3. Use Monitoring and Alerting:

Monitoring MySQL database servers is essential to detect and resolve potential issues that can affect performance, availability or security.

Manual monitoring can be tedious and prone to errors, hence using monitoring tools can help. Monitoring tools can track server metrics such as CPU usage, memory usage, database connections, replication status, and server alerts. Alerting systems can be used to notify database administrators of critical issues, such as a server crash or the inability to perform backups.

4. Optimize Performance:

MySQL performance can significantly impact application performance. Automating performance tuning tasks using tools like Percona Toolkit can aid in finding out performance bottlenecks and suggest MySQL configuration adjustments. Tuning options like query optimization will reduce query time and help to balance server loads. Another set of optimization options to consider is server-area optimizations which consists of tweaks to the file system, network settings, and other non-trivial settings.

5. Use Security Automation:

Securing MySQL databases is crucial to protect the databases from unauthorized access and vulnerabilities. Securing MySQL includes tasks such as configuring access control, securing passwords, enabling SSL encryption and restricting network access. Security automation tools like MySQL SSL and Securich can be used to automate and enforce security best practices across MySQL servers.

In summary, automating operations and maintenance tasks in MySQL is essential for efficient, secure and reliable database management. Configuration management tools, backup and recovery automation, monitoring and alerting tools, performance optimization tools, and security automation tools are some of the best practices to consider while automating MySQL. These tools can provide consistency, reliability, scalability, efficiency and error-free environment in a MySQL environment.

6.16 How do you implement advanced backup and recovery strategies in MySQL, including incremental backups, point-in-time recovery, and delayed replication?

To implement advanced backup and recovery strategies in MySQL, we can use some practices like incremental backups, point-in-time recovery, and delayed replication.

Incremental Backups
Incremental backups allow us to only backup the data that has changed since the last backup, which reduces backup time and the amount of storage needed for backups. This can be performed using either physical or logical incremental backups.

- Physical Incremental Backups: This backs up the physical file changes on disk since the last backup, and it is faster and takes up less disk space than logical backups. Physical backups are performed using tools like 'Percona XtraBackup'.

- Logical Incremental Backups: This backs up the SQL statements that have been executed since the last backup, and it can capture data changes that are not reflected in the physical files like 'DDL' changes. However, it can be slower and requires more disk space than physical backups. Logical backups can be performed using tools like 'mysqldump'.

Point-in-Time Recovery
Point-in-time recovery allows us to restore the database to any point in time between backups, which is useful when we need to recover a database from a specific time or to recover from an error. To perform point-in-time recovery, we need to have a complete and consistent backup and a list of all the changes made to the database since the backup. This can be implemented using the following steps:

- Enable Binary logging: Binary logging is used to record all changes made to the database, which is needed to recover the database to a point in time.

- Take Full and incremental backups: Full database backups should be taken periodically and incremental backups should be taken regularly.

- Monitor the binary log: We need to monitor the binary log to track any changes made to the database.

- Restore from backup and replay the binary log: To perform point-in-time recovery, we need to restore from the last complete backup and replay the binary log up to the desired point in time.

Delayed Replication
Delayed replication allows us to replicate changes to a secondary database server after a delay, which can be useful in scenarios where we need to prevent data loss due to accidental data deletion or other errors. To implement delayed replication, we can use the following steps:

- Enable binary logging and set the 'slave-delay' parameter: We need to enable binary logging on the primary server and set the 'slave-delay' parameter on the secondary server.

- Start replication and apply the delay: We need to start replication and apply the delay by setting the appropriate value for 'slave-delay'.

- Monitor replication and apply corrective measures: We need to monitor replication and apply corrective measures if there are any issues with replication.

In summary, implementing advanced backup and recovery strategies in MySQL involves the use of incremental backups, point-in-time recovery, and delayed replication. These strategies can help to reduce backup time, minimize data loss, and recover quickly from errors. The choice of strategy depends on the specific use case and requirements.

6.17   Can you discuss the challenges and best practices for optimizing MySQL in virtualized and containerized environments, such as VMware, Docker, and Kubernetes?

There are several challenges to consider when optimizing MySQL in virtualized and containerized environments. In traditional environments, MySQL can be tuned to use specific hardware resources, whereas in virtualized environments, the resources are shared and can be restricted by the hypervisor. In containerized environments, MySQL must contend with container resource limits, network isolation, and issues related to ephemeral data storage. Here are some best practices for optimizing MySQL in virtualized and containerized environments.

1. Right-size the VM or container
Virtual machines and containers can be resized based on the workloads they handle. These can be upsized or downsized based on the amount of compute, network, and storage resources needed by the applications running on them. Right-sizing is crucial when tuning MySQL to allocate the right amount of memory and CPU resources.

2. Set and test performance thresholds
It is important to set performance thresholds for MySQL and test them under load. This allows for proper benchmarking and validation of the virtualized environment. Additionally, it helps prevent bottlenecks, network delays, and other performance issues. It is important to test the system under realistic loads, ensuring that MySQL performance remains consistent.

3. Use InnoDB as a storage engine
InnoDB is the default storage engine for MySQL, and it is ideal for virtualized environments. Its row-level locking capabilities ensure high concurrency and allow for optimization of resource utilization. Additionally, InnoDB has built-in resilience features such as real-time replication, backups and data integrity checks that assist with high availability (HA) setups.

4. Minimize network latency
In virtualized or containerized environments, network latency is a primary cause of poor performance. Containers and VMs can be spread out over physical servers in a virtualized environment or hosts in Kubernetes. Additionally, storage access can also impact network latency, especially when disk I/O is bottlenecked. The use of distributed/replicated storage systems like GlusterFS and Ceph or a shared file system like NFS, can provide better storage performance across nodes in the virtualized environment.

5. Use MySQL-specific tools to optimize performance
MySQL has several built-in tools that can help optimize performance

in virtualized environments. These include tools like 'EXPLAIN'
for analyzing slow queries, 'pt-query-digest' for query profiling, and
'mysqlslap' for benchmarking MySQL under various workloads. MySQL
performance can also be monitored using third-party tools like Prometheus
or New Relic, which can provide real-time performance data and
alerts.

6. Tune MySQL settings for virtualization
MySQL settings need to be tuned to work in virtualized environments.
Tuning database options should be done based on the virtualization
technology being used. MySQL configuration should be set according
to the available hardware resources.

7. Regularly test and optimize performance
Finally, continuous performance testing and optimization are essential for maintaining optimal performance in virtualized environments.
DBAs should regularly re-test performance bottlenecks and modify
resource allocation and system settings to address deficiencies. Additionally, it is vital to follow industry-leading practices in this regard.

By following these best practices and optimizing the MySQL database
for virtualized and containerized environments, DBAs can ensure consistent performance of their applications.

6.18 How do you manage and optimize MySQL deployments in hybrid trans-actional and analytical processing (HTAP) scenarios, balancing the needs of OLTP and OLAP workloads?

Hybrid Transactional and Analytical Processing (HTAP) is an emerging data processing model that combines Online Transaction Processing (OLTP) and Online Analytical Processing (OLAP) workloads in
the same database system. In the context of MySQL, managing and
optimizing HTAP deployments involves balancing the needs of OLTP
and OLAP workloads, ensuring efficient utilization of hardware resources, and minimizing data latency.

Here are some best practices for managing and optimizing MySQL deployments in HTAP scenarios:

1. Use a columnar storage engine for OLAP workloads: MySQL supports both row-based and columnar storage engines. Row-based storage is optimized for OLTP workloads, where data is primarily accessed row by row. However, columnar storage is optimized for OLAP workloads, where data is primarily accessed column by column. Using a columnar storage engine, such as InnoDB or MyRocks, can significantly improve the performance of OLAP workloads.

2. Use partitioning to manage large tables: Partitioning is a technique that involves dividing a large table into smaller, more manageable partitions. Each partition can be stored on a separate physical location, allowing for parallel processing and improved performance. Partitioning can also help to manage the storage requirements of large tables, as well as improve query response times.

3. Use indexing to improve query performance: Indexing is a technique that involves creating indexes on columns that are frequently used in queries. Indexes help to speed up query execution by allowing the database to quickly locate the relevant data. However, indexing can also slow down data modifications (such as INSERT, UPDATE, and DELETE operations), so it is important to use indexing judiciously.

4. Optimize hardware resources: HTAP workloads can be resource-intensive, requiring a significant amount of CPU, memory, and storage. To optimize hardware resources, consider using a high-performance storage subsystem (such as solid-state drives), adding more memory to the system, and using multiple processors or cores.

5. Use caching to improve performance: Caching is a technique that involves storing frequently accessed data in memory. MySQL supports several caching mechanisms, including query cache and InnoDB buffer pool. Caching can help to improve query performance, reduce data access latency, and minimize the load on the storage subsystem.

6. Use workload management tools: Workload management tools, such as MySQL Enterprise Monitor, can help to monitor and optimize MySQL deployments in HTAP scenarios. These tools can provide insights into the performance of individual queries, as well as identify

potential bottlenecks and areas for optimization.

In summary, managing and optimizing MySQL deployments in HTAP scenarios involves balancing the needs of OLTP and OLAP workloads, optimizing hardware resources, and using best practices such as columnar storage, partitioning, indexing, caching, and workload management tools.

6.19 What are the key considerations when integrating MySQL with big data and machine learning technologies, such as Hadoop, Apache Spark, or TensorFlow?

There are several key considerations when integrating MySQL with big data and machine learning technologies. Here are some of the most important ones:

1. Data transfer: Since MySQL is a relational database, it may not be the best tool for processing and storing big data. To take advantage of big data technologies like Hadoop, Apache Spark, or TensorFlow, you may need to transfer your data from MySQL to a big data platform. This can be done using data integration tools like Sqoop, which can move data between MySQL and Hadoop or Spark.

2. Data storage: Hadoop and Spark use distributed file systems to store data, whereas TensorFlow relies on data being stored in memory. This means you may need to restructure your data to fit the storage requirements of these technologies. For example, you may need to convert your data to a file format like Parquet or Avro to store it in Hadoop or Spark. Alternatively, you may need to move your data to a NoSQL database like MongoDB or Cassandra that can handle unstructured data.

3. Data processing: Big data and machine learning technologies are designed to handle large volumes of data and complex analysis tasks. This means you may need to rethink your data processing workflows to take advantage of these tools. For example, you might use Apache

Spark to run complex machine learning algorithms on your data, or use TensorFlow to build and train deep neural networks.

4. Scalability: One of the primary benefits of big data and machine learning technologies is their scalability. However, this also means you need to design your systems to scale effectively. For example, you may need to use tools like Apache Kafka to handle high volumes of data in real time, or use Kubernetes to manage and orchestrate your big data and machine learning workloads.

5. Performance: When working with big data and machine learning technologies, performance can be a critical concern. This means you need to optimize your systems to run efficiently and minimize resource usage. For example, you might use caching and indexing to speed up queries in MySQL, or use techniques like data sharding and partitioning to distribute your data across multiple nodes in your big data cluster.

Overall, integrating MySQL with big data and machine learning technologies requires careful planning and consideration. By focusing on data transfer, storage, processing, scalability, and performance, you can build systems that handle large volumes of data and run complex analysis tasks efficiently and effectively.

6.20   Can you share your experience and insights on contributing to the MySQL open-source community, including bug reporting, feature development, and knowledge sharing?

MySQL is one of the most popular open-source relational database management systems in use today. It is developed, distributed, and supported by Oracle Corporation. The MySQL community is a diverse group of users, developers, and enthusiasts who collaborate to improve the software, fix bugs, develop new features, and share knowledge and best practices.

Here are some ways to contribute to the MySQL open-source community:

1. Bug reporting: If you find a bug in MySQL or any other open-source software, you can report it to the development team using the bug tracking system. This helps the developers to identify and fix the bug, and improve the quality of the software.

2. Feature development: MySQL is an open-source software, which means that anyone can contribute code to the project, subject to certain guidelines and processes. If you have an idea for a new feature or improvement to the software, you can propose it to the community, and if it is accepted, you can work on implementing it.

3. Code review: MySQL is a complex software with millions of lines of code. The development team relies on code reviews to ensure that new code is of high quality, follows best practices, and does not break existing functionality. You can participate in code reviews and provide feedback and suggestions to the developers.

4. Knowledge sharing: MySQL has a vibrant community of users and developers who share their knowledge and expertise through forums, blogs, and other platforms. You can contribute by writing articles, giving presentations, or answering questions in the forums.

5. Testing: When new versions of MySQL are released, they need to be thoroughly tested to ensure that they are stable, performant, and compatible with existing software. You can participate in the testing process by downloading the software, running tests, and reporting any issues you encounter.

In conclusion, contributing to the MySQL open-source community is a rewarding experience that can help you improve your skills, build your reputation, and make a positive impact on the software and the community.